Symbol of wisdom and learning, the owl of Minerva (shown above on an ancient Greek coin) was recently adopted as the badge of office of the Secretary of the Smithsonian.

THE SMITHSONIAN INSTITUTION

an establishment for the increase & diffusion of Knowledge among men.

NARRATIVE BY

WALTER KARP

PUBLISHED BY

THE SMITHSONIAN INSTITUTION

IN ASSOCIATION WITH

THE EDITORS OF AMERICAN HERITAGE MAGAZINE

A HANDBOOK TO THE National Museum AT THE Smithsonian Institution Washington.

The title page above is taken from a nineteenth-century Smithsonian guide.

Table of Contents

CHAPTER ONE   THE LEGACY   7

John Quincy Adams:
Guarding the Trust   16

The First Secretary
And His "Philosophical Toys"   24

CHAPTER TWO   NATURAL HISTORY   29

John Wesley Powell:
Founding the B.A.E.   40

A Living Museum   50

CHAPTER THREE   FLIGHT, SPACE, AND THE ELEMENTS   55

Samuel Pierpont Langley:
Toward a New Astronomy   62

Sunlight
And the Secrets of Life   70

CHAPTER FOUR   A HISTORY WRITTEN IN OBJECTS   75

George Brown Goode:
Building a "House Full of Ideas"   80

Miniature Mementos
Of Yankee Inventiveness   90

CHAPTER FIVE   THE ARTS   95

Andrew W. Mellon:
Acquiring a Taste for the Finest   104

Ancient Art
From the Orient   114

CHAPTER SIX   THE SOCIETY OF SCHOLARS   119

INDEX AND ACKNOWLEDGMENTS   126

Chapter One

THE LEGACY

There is no simple way to describe the Smithsonian Institution. It includes one of the world's greatest museum complexes, but it is far more than a museum. It receives a part of its support from the United States Congress, but it is not a Government agency. Even to say the Smithsonian is located in Washington, D.C., is not altogether correct. The Smithsonian banner is permanently aloft as well in a special jungle preserve in Panama; at the headquarters of the River Basin Surveys in Lincoln, Nebraska; and in an astrophysical observatory in Cambridge, Massachusetts. The Institution, with its dazzlingly varied collections, seems to be the product of a passion for facts and things; in its research staff, working out of sight in building wings and tantalizingly closed-off corridors, it is intent upon naming, classifying, and systematizing. The Smithsonian itself resists classification.

Yet, if the Institution has no simple label, what it possesses instead is a rich, kaleidoscopic history. It is equally the child of science, of adventure, and of America's fortunes through more than a century of growth and change.

The story of the Smithsonian begins in the nineteenth century, tinged with melodrama the way novels from that era so often begin—with a noble family, an illicit birth, and a first chapter that might well be called "The Mysterious Bequest."

In the year 1835, when Andrew Jackson was President of twenty-four United States and 15,000,000 people, America's diplomatic officer in London sent back strange tidings to his chief in Washington. Some Englishman, he had just been informed, had left more than £100,000 to the United States of America. His name was James Smithson, which meant nothing in Washington, for nobody there had ever heard of him. Smithson himself, authorities learned, had never been to America, had no friends in America, nor any known American friends abroad. Understandably, the chargé d'affaires recorded in his note his own suspicion that the testator might have been temporarily insane. Men who leave sizable fortunes to governments under any circumstances are unusual, but a man who gives money to a government and a nation with which he has no apparent personal connection may well be accounted exceedingly odd. His one known tie to the United States turned out to be no tie at all: His half-brother, Lord Percy, had commanded British troops at the Battle of Lexington and there had saved the beaten redcoats from utter rout—scarcely

Born into the era of the Enlightenment, James Smithson was raised at a time when science was the concern of everybody, including children. At left, Joseph Wright's painting of a household lecture about the solar system, in which a lamp is used to represent the sun, suggests the spirit of an age enthralled by scientific investigation. Above, the allegorical frontispiece to Sprat's History of the Royal Society, *that prestigious fraternity of scholars which Smithson later was to join, records the ascendancy of experimental science by portraying, at right, the great empiricist Francis Bacon and, behind Bacon, a panel of scientific instruments.*

As a young man attending Oxford, Smithson wears his academic cap and gown. An unknown artist painted his portrait in 1786, the year he graduated.

a positive contribution to America's national development. Nonetheless, there was the will, proud and terse, almost disastrously terse as it turned out. "I James Smithson," it began, "Son to Hugh, first Duke of Northumberland, & Elizabeth, Heiress of the Hungerfords of Studley, & Niece to Charles the Proud Duke of Somerset. . . ." His lineage traced, Smithson then stipulated that his fortune was to go to his nephew, and should his nephew die without heirs (which he did in 1835—had he not, the Smithsonian Institution would have been just a family anecdote), "I then bequeath the whole of my property . . . to the United States of America, to found at Washington, under the name to the Smithsonian institution, an establishment for the increase & diffusion of Knowledge among men." There was not a word more, either to describe further the curious institution he had in mind or to explain his reasons for leaving a fortune to a distant republic he had never seen.

Definitely, America's benefactor was a strange man, and many people have been baffled since by his motives, including, as it soon turned out, the Congress of the United States. Today, however, with the kind help of hindsight, the circuitous path leading up to Smithson's will seems to have been almost foreordained.

James Smithson was born in France in 1765, a decade before the United States was born with "the shot heard round the world." His father was Sir Hugh Smithson, who in 1766 became the first Duke of Northumberland. His mother was Elizabeth Hungerford Keate Macie, the wealthy widowed cousin of Sir Hugh's own wife. James Smithson, in short, was illegitimate. Lest this conjure up images of abandonment, poverty, and foundling homes, it is worth recalling that to be the illegitimate son of a wealthy peer and an aristocratic heiress was no crushing burden in those days. To be sure, it cut Smithson off from any of the family's half-dozen noble titles. Doubtless, it cut him off also from the loftier reaches of aristocratic society. But in 1782 history next reveals Smithson enrolled with all the signs of affluence as a gentleman-commoner of Pembroke College, Oxford, under his mother's name of Macie. Until his mother's death many years later, it was the name by which he would be known. He was a slender, serious young man with a taste for mineralogy strong enough to inspire a rock-collecting tour of the wilds of Scotland's Western Islands. Such gentlemanly rock collecting was by no

Revolutionary patriots, at right, gleefully topple a gilded statue of George III, in a painting by William Walcutt. In 1789 Charles Willson Peale painted the portrait above of Benjamin Franklin—including the statesman's writings and quill pen, and a bolt of lightning representing Franklin's experiments in electricity. A land of liberty, where politicians took an interest in science, America seemed to young Europeans like Smithson a place where learning could flourish in freedom. The influence of the new country was strongly felt. George Washington had urged in his Farewell Address, with words oddly evocative of Smithson's will, that Americans build "institutions for the general diffusion of knowledge."

means an oddity in the eighteenth century. Indeed, an amateur's interest in science was then considered a fine ornament for a serious gentleman. Thomas Jefferson was such an amateur natural historian—ardent enough, in fact, to reserve one room in the White House for examining fossil bones. But young Smithson went one giant step further: He decided to devote his life to chemistry and mineralogy, fully and professionally. He wanted nothing less than to leave his name in the pantheon of science. He had every reason to think he might. Chemistry, bursting suddenly into prominence, was the most exciting science of the day. In 1766 Henry Cavendish had presented the first of his famous papers on the chemistry of gases to the Royal Society. In 1774 Joseph Priestley had discovered dephlogisticated air, or oxygen. In 1787, a year after Smithson was graduated from Oxford, the great Frenchman Antoine Lavoisier had overturned a hundred years of chemical theorizing by debunking the phlogistic doctrine, and set the world's chemists rushing ahead on the right path. There were discoveries to be made on every hand and James Smithson expected to share in making them. Learned circles were happy to welcome him. In 1788, at the age of twenty-three, he was named

a Fellow of the Royal Society of London, the world's pre-eminent society of scientists. Henry Cavendish, a fellow aristocrat, was one of his sponsors. Just four years later Smithson was sufficiently advanced in his chosen field to read an original paper before that august body. It was a modest effort, an analysis of the chemical composition of an exotic substance found in bamboo. Nevertheless, his hopes ran high. "My name," he later vowed, "shall live in the memory of man when the titles of the Northumberlands and Percys are extinct and forgotten."

There was more than vainglory in that resounding vow. Never before in history had noble titles seemed, at least to liberal young men like Smithson, so close to the point of extinction. Stirred by the American Revolution, a profound passion for reform, for liberty, and for learning was sweeping Europe. Never was a period so optimistic as in those days of Smithson's youth, the days of the Enlightenment. Educate the masses, publish scientific encyclopedias, and overthrow kings, ran the stirring message, and liberty, justice, and reason would soon prevail. Among the enlightened of Europe, George Washington and Benjamin Franklin were proudly singled out to the skeptics. Were they not living

proof that a republic produced a higher type of man than a monarchy? When the poet Joel Barlow, America's ambassador to Paris, unfolded his vision of an "Athens rising on the banks of the Potomac," Europeans were prepared to listen. Then the French Revolution broke out in 1789, raising optimism to dizzying heights. "Bliss was it in that dawn to be alive," wrote the poet William Wordsworth, "but to be young was very Heaven!"

And Smithson was young. In 1792, when the king of France was drawing close to the guillotine, Smithson, aged twenty-seven, was in Paris, cheering on the Revolution. "Things are going on," he exclaimed in a letter to an Oxford friend. "Stupidity and guilt have had a long reign, and it begins indeed to be the time for justice and common sense to have their term." Monarchy, he told his friend, "[is] a contemptible incumbrance." He himself, to use his phrase, was "of the democratic party." Whether he remained of that radical party in later years no one is certain, but for nearly all the rest of his life, Paris, the revolutionary city par excellence, became his headquarters.

In the meantime, Smithson's chemical researches continued in his private laboratory. He had become a student of analytical chemistry. Skillfully and elegantly he employed the crude tests then available to determine the exact composition of a remarkable variety of substances, from Vesuvius lava to artichokes. On his travels he would carry a portable laboratory for on-the-spot analyses of any curious morsel of matter he encountered along the way. Once, he told a friend, upon seeing a tear trickle down a lady's cheek, he rushed to catch it in a vial. Bringing it back to his laboratory, he extracted four kinds of salt from it. There was nothing amateurish about Smithson's work: The best English scientific journals published his papers. He had to his credit the identification of a new mineral ore now known as smithsonite. But real fame eluded him. Science is stingy with its laurels. The immortality Smithson craved, science reserves only for its great discoverers—and Smithson, for all his skill and intelligence, was not of that rank.

The years passed; his health began to fade, and with it his hopes. Aside from science, he had little to show for his life. He was a man without a family and without a country, "the distinguished foreigner of great wealth" who circulated about Europe and knew all the great scientists whose work surpassed his own. Late in life he

under the name to the Smithsonian institution, an establishment for the increase & diffusion of knowledge among men.

Smithson, above in a small medallion portrait, gave his fortune to America, with only the barest hint of what the country was to do with it. The brief passage from Smithson's will, at top, was the only writing he left to indicate his intent, and Congress debated its meaning for fully a decade. At right, in a photograph taken later from a tower of the completed Smithsonian Building, the Capitol rises above the old Mall.

took to spending half his day in his study with his researches and the other half at the gaming tables.

In the year 1826 he was back in London again. He was sixty-one years old, and the name that he had hoped to perpetuate was about to die with him. What had not died, we may conjecture, was the old spirit of the Enlightenment years. The advancement of learning, that was the great thing; and Smithson never doubted it, for he had never ceased his own experimental work, not even in the depths of his disappointment. If not he, then other investigators in his name might add to human knowledge. And why not in America where there was no such "contemptible incumbrance" as a king? Had not his fellow chemist Joseph Priestley declared that greater discoveries would be made in a republic than in a monarchy? Had not America's own President Jefferson protected Priestley after the British had hounded him into exile for his political beliefs? The future was with America, and Smithson decided to join his destiny to it. On October 23, 1826, he sat down to make his last will and testament. Three years later the wandering chemist died and was buried in a tiny English cemetery in Genoa, Italy. In 1835 his nephew died without an heir, and so Smithson's fortune

passed, in accord with the terms of his will, to the United States.

Today it is hard to imagine how a half-million-dollar gift could become, in the space of ten years, a constitutional challenge, a vexing problem, and then a public scandal, but that is exactly what happened to Smithson's money. During those years anyone wagering that the bequest would eventually be put to good use could justly be set down as a die-hard optimist. The problem of devising an institution to increase and diffuse knowledge among men was put into the hands of Congress, and Congress was laboring in a vacuum. In 1835 Joel Barlow's Athens-on-the-Potomac was a mud-splattered village of little more than 40,000 citizens, 48 Senators, and 256 Congressmen. It was trying hard to lead a nation that had grown intensely busy and intensely practical. Perhaps at no time in the capital's history was it ever less like ancient Athens or less interested in institutions for increasing and diffusing knowledge. Indeed, the first Congressional response to Smithson's bequest was the demand by a minority of Senators that the legacy be refused outright. According to John C. Calhoun, it was "beneath the dignity of the country to accept such gifts from foreigners." The golden dream of a republic of virtue and enlightenment governed by pa-

trons of science and learning had grown dim with the death, one by one, of the Founding Fathers.

As for science, Congress had little opportunity to appreciate it in 1835. To be sure, there was considerable display of "Yankee inventiveness" and mechanical tinkering in America at that time, but scientific research was practically nonexistent. There were no scientific schools, few full-time scientists, and barely a handful of institutions of higher learning of any kind. In science, America was the humble student of Europe. As the one great American physicist of the day put it: "Every man who can burn phosphorus in oxygen and exhibit a few experiments to a class of young ladies is called a man of science." (Fortunately, that outspoken physicist was to become the first head of the Smithsonian.) Clearly, a Smithsonian Institution was desperately needed, but what sort of institution should it be? What, after all, did "increase of knowledge" mean? According to one Congressman, if a man taught his neighbor something the neighbor did not know, *that* increased knowledge. Even Daniel Webster argued that increase and diffusion were two words with the same meaning. Whatever the phrase meant, on July 1, 1838, Congress authorized the President to appoint an agent to

journey to England to collect the money, and, in August, 1838, 105 bags of gold sovereigns, worth precisely $508,318.46 at the United States Mint, arrived by packet boat in New York.

The Congressional debate then began in earnest—its confused, eight-year course conducted under the watchful eye of former President John Quincy Adams. At the age of sixty-four, Adams had returned to the House with a faith in his colleagues that was small indeed. Unless Congress were watched, Adams told a friend, the great bequest "will be squandered on cormorants or wasted in electioneering bribery." Determinedly, he made himself the protector of the all-too-vulnerable Smithsonian money (see p. 16). But, as the debate dragged on, Adams grew almost frantic with fear that neglect and mischief would gobble up the legacy before anything at all was accomplished. After two years of discussion, Congress succeeded in making only one firm decision. It took the Smithsonian fund out of the United States Treasury and invested most of it in Arkansas state bonds—which promptly defaulted. "The fangs of the state of Arkansas," Adams complained in private.

Honorable men as well as schemers cast their eyes on Smithson's legacy. In 1840 a private organization was formed that did more

Founded in a period of scientific illiteracy, the Smithsonian grew up with the emergence of bright American inventors. Thomas Edison, at right with his wax-cylinder phonograph, was born in 1847, the year after the Smithsonian was established. Before his death he took out 1,093 patents (more than any other man) from the U.S. Patent Office, including those for his phonograph, and the incandescent lamp above. Such energetic innovation—with the Smithsonian's pure research leading to ever more advanced ideas—soon gave America one of the most sophisticated scientific communities in the world.

than any legislator to influence the future of the still unborn Smithsonian. Joel Poinsett, Secretary of War and amateur naturalist (the poinsettia bears his name), organized among Washington's distinguished citizens a group known as the National Institution for the Promotion of Science (later named the National Institute). Its chief means for promoting science was to be a large museum of natural history. Its immediate objective was to win control over Smithson's money and over the natural history specimens brought back from the South Seas by the government-supported Wilkes Expedition in 1842. Politically astute and influential, the group obtained informal custody of the collections that same year. Then quite as suddenly, Congress grew suspicious of the fast-moving institute, and during the next several years the institute lost ground steadily.

In the Congressional debates of 1845, William Allen of Ohio treated the institute to a sarcastic roasting. "This association . . . finding a Capitol here and a public Treasury here," Allen said, "called itself a National Institute." Then, to legalize its claim to "that pompous title," it tried to win "the exclusive administration of half a million of the public money." The organization was unknown to the Constitution of the United States, Allen declared;

and, shortly after his attack, the name of the institute disappeared from Congressional debate. But it left its indelible mark on the amorphous Congressional debate and on the ultimate form of the Smithsonian: A museum, hitherto unmentioned, became another piece in the perplexing jigsaw puzzle.

By 1845 "the Smithsonian Problem" was fast becoming "the Smithsonian Scandal"—"a curse, a burning sin," exclaimed one Senator. Seven years had passed and Congress was still at loggerheads. Just before Christmas of 1844, Senator Benjamin Tappen of Ohio offered a plan of an exceedingly practical kind: The Smithsonian was to be made into an experimental agriculture station with some professors attached to it to teach young men navigation, house building, and animal husbandry. After the Christmas recess, Senator Rufus Choate of Massachusetts rose to sneer at Tappen for his "narrow utilitarianism." Choate, a learned jurist and avid bibliophile, proposed instead in his magniloquent way "a various and ample library. . .durable as liberty, durable as the Union; a vast storehouse, a vast treasury, of all the facts which make up the history of man and of nature. . . ." Later, in the House, Robert Dale Owen of Indiana, son of the great British Utopian reformer Robert

Joseph Henry's Yale electromagnet, at right in a small-scale replica, was designed in 1831, and lifted over a ton.

Bell's telephone receiver, below, was first exhibited to the public at the Philadelphia Centennial Exposition of 1876.

The simple sewing machine above was invented by Elias Howe in 1845, and was soon sold to an English corsetier for £250.

Owen, delivered his opinion of grand libraries: "petty antiquarian triumphs" and "clouds of windy verbiage." Owen then proposed an institution that would include a natural history collection, a laboratory, a garden for farm experiments, and, most important of all in his eyes, a "normal school" for training teachers in the practical arts and elementary sciences. The next day, Congressman G. P. Marsh of Vermont, another strong library advocate, rose to answer Owen: "Sir, a laboratory is a charnel house."

At last, in August, 1846, Congress agreed that it would never really agree, and it produced an act of establishment that incorporated a little of everything. The Smithsonian Institution was to be governed by a Board of Regents composed of the Chief Justice of the United States, the Vice-President, three Congressmen, three Senators, and six private citizens—the composition of the Board of Regents to this day. It was to begin by erecting a building "of plain and durable materials and structure, without unnecessary ornament" to house a museum, a study collection of scientific materials gathered by the United States Government, a chemical laboratory, a library, a gallery of art, and lecture rooms. All this was to be accomplished solely on the income from the legacy—$30,000 a year (6 per cent of

the half million dollars held by the Treasury). The principal—this was Adams's policy—was not to be touched. Any money left over, Congress declared, could be used by the Regents to promote "the purpose of the testator" as they saw fit.

In truth, had Congress demanded strict obedience to its requirements, the Smithsonian Institution would have sunk under its burdens without a trace. Wisely, Congress was not so pertinacious, and equally wisely, the Board of Regents took advantage of the freedom they were given.

Led by Robert Dale Owen, who was convinced that only a large and dignified structure would lend substance to the shadowy Institution, the Regents quickly allocated the munificent sum of "$242,000 to erect a building," this sum being the amount of interest the Smithsonian fund had accumulated during eight years of debating. Congress had stipulated no "unnecessary ornament," but the Board's building committee, under Owen, had other ideas. After visiting such edifices as the Boston Masonic Temple, the New Jersey State Lunatic Asylum, and the Eastern Penitentiary, the committee turned to James Renwick, Jr., designer of New York's Grace Church (and, later, of St. Patrick's Cathedral). Renwick's scheme for a plain

CONTINUED ON PAGE 19

John Quincy Adams:
Guarding the Trust

Throughout the Congressional debates over James Smithson's bequest, one man consistently understood its significance. "But so little are the feelings of others in unison with mine . . . ," John Quincy Adams confided to his diary, "that no one thinks of attributing it to a benevolent motive." The Representative from Massachusetts knew better. Indeed, in all America there was not a single man of government more sensitively attuned to the spare language of Smithson's will than this aging former President, whose daguerreotype portrait is at right. Son of the second President of the United States, Congressman Adams had passed more than a third of his first forty years overseas, in Continental academies, accompanying his father, and as a diplomat himself. His was a transatlantic education, a grand tour lasting half his life, making the earnest Yankee Puritan a child of the Enlightenment as well. Just two years younger than James Smithson, he was himself an apostle of the light of reason.

Like Smithson, too, he was a scientist. As a young man he had singled out the life of science as "the most honourable avenue to the temple of fame," and by old age he could point to at least one solid achievement—a thick monograph on weights and measures, compiled while he was Secretary of State. But there were other interests which, if less sustained, were also less forbidding. From breeding butterflies to watching stars, science was an intense, absorbing hobby. Years later his grandson Henry would recall how the old man harassed his fragile wife by carrying off to his dressing closet her finest cut-glass bowls, in which he would plant acorns and observe their growth.

Above all, he was fond of astronomy, and it was to this passion that he turned when the time came to propose a use for Smithson's fortune. Smithson, he conceded, had never been an astronomer, yet Adams was untroubled by so slight an infidelity. "The express object of an observatory," he proclaimed, "is the increase of knowledge by new discovery." And this endeavor was precisely what the words of Smithson's will meant to him.

In the end, by the last session of the Smithsonian debates, he was ready to abandon his plan for an observatory—but not the policy behind it. When Robert Dale Owen reported a bill that urged the construction of a normal school, an institution to train teachers, Adams was aghast. Nothing, he felt sure, was more remote from Smithson's aims than simple education, "the communication of knowledge already possessed," and so the old man made one last great effort. He would rather see "the whole money thrown into the Potomac," he told his colleagues, than to spend a single dollar on a normal school. And with that caustic remark, he finally made his point. By a vote of 72 to 42, the House approved his motion to strike the provision for a school, and John Quincy Adams cast his vote for what remained: the bill setting up the Smithsonian as it finally came to be, without an observatory.

If he could not have his own way entirely, at least the trust was not betrayed—and the infant Institution would have a chance, given dedicated leadership, to justify the brilliant sense of exultation that ten years earlier he had given voice to in his first report on Smithson's gift: ". . . to what higher or nobler object could this generous and splendid donation have been devoted?" The purpose of Smithson's gift, as Adams persistently interpreted it through the years of debate, was to expand the total store of human knowledge. Although he had lost his cherished observatory, he had made certain that the pursuit of "new discovery"—original research—would be an inextricable part of the Smithsonian.

James Renwick's controversial building, opposite, was photographed by A. J. Russell in 1862.

Senator Rufus Choate, left, wanted Smithson's money used to construct "a various and ample library." All that was necessary, he said, was "a plain, spacious, fireproof building; a librarian and assistants; an agent to buy your books; and a fire to sit by." As it turned out, though, he was disappointed. His library was whittled down, to the point where he indignantly resigned from the Smithsonian's Board of Regents. And the simple building he had hoped for became, instead, an elaborate medieval castle.

A vast, impressive structure was what fragile Robert Dale Owen, left, thought the Smithsonian should have to make its presence conspicuous to the nation as a whole. As a Regent of the Institution, he played an important role in selecting Renwick's Norman design, and supervised the construction of the building. The architect, he said happily, had improved on "ancient precedents . . . with discretion and advantage," and had begun to evolve a new "National Style of Architecture for America."

CONTINUED FROM PAGE 15

building was based on the style of the twelfth-century Norman castles. In addition to nine towers and campaniles, Renwick's building had enough niches, traceries, and chapel-like rooms to suggest that the architect had not quite shaken his preoccupation with cathedral building. On May 1, 1847, the cornerstone for the Smithsonian Building was laid at a gala public ceremony preceded by a parade of local dignitaries, along with the local militia and the local Freemasons. (To reach the site, the marchers did not cross the neat grassy Mall as it is today, but rather an unkempt field traversed by an open sewer known euphemistically as the Canal.) By 1855, after vexing delays, the building was substantially finished; and neither the somewhat remote location a mile from the center of town nor the unsavory surroundings could diminish Washington's pride in the oddly romantic red stone castle that looked so magnificent in a town of wooden houses and unpaved streets.

But a building is not a policy, and in the very same month that the Regents had decided to build a castle they still had not figured out what the people in the castle were supposed to do. A long delay would probably have proven fatal, for the Smithsonian was a defenseless creature in a hotbed of politics. Most voters in the country

did not know or care about it; most Congressmen were indifferent or even hostile. As if to underscore that fact, Congressman Andrew Johnson of Tennessee began accusing the Smithsonian of "sucking the blood" from the taxpayer, because the Treasury paid the Smithsonian 6 per cent interest; and, in 1848, he proposed that Congress turn it into a school "for the orphan children of Washington, D.C." But that was only a menacing gesture. Much later, in 1852, Stephen A. Douglas, "the Little Giant," was to try a real raid on the Smithsonian. Seeking to woo the rural vote, he proposed, innocently enough, the formation of an agricultural bureau to aid the farmer. What was more, he told farmers, it would not cost the taxpayer a cent: James Smithson's money would pay for it. The Smithsonian must have looked like rather easy prey. When Rufus Choate and G. P. Marsh, the two former advocates in Congress of the library plan, became Smithsonian Regents, they had every intention of turning the Institution into a library before many years had passed. Who would be able to resist them?

Fortunately that question was resolved in December of 1846: By the narrow margin of a 7 to 5 vote, the Board of Regents elected a forty-six-year-old Princeton professor of science named Joseph Henry

as the first Secretary of the Smithsonian Institution (the title of the Institution's executive head). It was the most important decision in the Smithsonian's history. Whatever designs anyone had upon the Smithsonian, from that day forward he had to deal with a formidable adversary. He had to deal, too, with an organization suddenly bursting with life and purpose. A month after Henry's election, and on his advice, the Board of Regents proclaimed as a fundamental tenet of policy an idea almost nobody had grasped in ten years of discussion: "The increase of knowledge by original research shall form an essential function" of the Smithsonian Institution. The Smithsonian was to be above all an active, professional scientific organization, the first of its kind in America. The diffusion of knowledge would have as its mainstay the publication and distribution of the results of original research. That, in brief, was Henry's plan; and today, more than a century later, research and publication remain essential aspects of the Smithsonian's complex role.

Soon enough one Congressman grumbled that there were certain "zealots for discovery" running the Smithsonian, but Henry had set the new, unfamiliar machinery in motion so quickly it was not easily stopped. By 1848 the Smithsonian had published its first learned

scientific work, the opening volume of what was to become a superb series known as *Smithsonian Contributions to Knowledge*. He took the initial steps toward establishing a far-flung system of Smithsonian volunteer weather observers that one day would form the basis of the United States Weather Bureau. Guidance, information, small sums of money, and scientific instruments quickly began to flow from the Smithsonian for the use of a rising generation of young American scientists. Within a year of its founding, the Smithsonian under Henry had become the focal point of American researchers. Its days of isolation and neglect were at an end. "I have succeeded," Henry wrote home to his wife from Washington, "beyond my most sanguine expectations in molding the opinions of the Board of Regents into that of my plan."

Henry had every reason to be surprised. Ordinarily, college professors do not easily mold the thoughts of Supreme Court Justices and United States Senators. But then Joseph Henry was no ordinary professor. In the entire history of American science the country has rarely produced his equal as a physicist. As a young schoolteacher in Albany, New York, experimenting in his spare time, Henry had discovered one of the most profound truths in science: the inter-

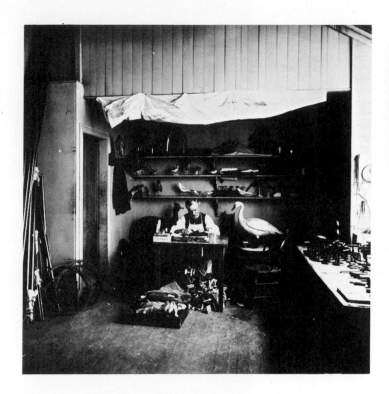

The community of scholars that gathered in the old Smithsonian was given bed and board as well as scientific facilities. At left, a taxidermist labors in an early laboratory. Bedrooms of the type above were allotted to young researchers who made the Institution crackle with their lively evening talk.

Secretary Henry, at left beside a volume of Smithsonian Contributions to Knowledge, *resided with his family for twenty-three years in Renwick's commodious building.*

changeability of magnetism and electricity, then known as the mysterious power of galvanism. Continuing his research, he built the world's first powerful electromagnet, virtually its first electric motor, and its first electromagnetic telegraph, all in the space of some six years of part-time research while he was in his early thirties. If he is little known by laymen today, it is because of a personal misfortune that probably constitutes the professional scientist's most common nightmare. The immortal Michael Faraday, working independently in England, made many of the same discoveries that Henry did—and, more importantly, published them first. The laurels went to the Englishman, Henry's investigations being considered but brilliant confirmations of Faraday's research. In public, Henry never complained, but no one knew better than he the price America's scientists were paying for the lack of journals in which to publish their work. Though he was reluctant to leave Princeton, the chance to make the Smithsonian an active friend and promoter of American science persuaded Henry to agree to head the new Institution. It was his duty, he said, "to prevent it from falling into worse hands."

The Smithsonian could not have found a better leader. Not only was Henry America's pre-eminent scientist, but he was himself

Joseph Henry, standing at the center, his elbow resting on a book, is surrounded by scientists and inventors of the nineteenth century in Christian Schussele's painting "Men of Progress," at right. From left to right, Henry's contemporaries include: Dr. William Morton, first man to demonstrate the use of ether; James Bogardus, innovator in factory building; Samuel Colt; Cyrus McCormick; Joseph Saxton, curator of standard balances for the U.S. Mint; Peter Cooper (pointing to the telegraph on the table); Charles Goodyear (in front of Cooper); Jordan Mott, builder of first anthracite coal cooking stoves; Eliphalet Nott, innovator with stoves; John Ericsson, designer of the Monitor; *Frederick Sickels, inventor of steering mechanisms for ships; Samuel F. B. Morse; Henry Burden, inventor of the railroad spike; Richard Hoe, developer of rotary printing presses; Erastus Brigham Bigelow, inventor of textile power looms; Isaiah Jennings, inventor of the threshing machine and other devices; Thomas Blanchard, developer of machine tools; and Elias Howe, inventor of the sewing machine. Of the entire group, only Henry was a research scientist. Yet, between the time of the Smithsonian's founding and the year 1862, when this painting was finished, science had progressed markedly in America.*

science's best advertisement. To a remarkable degree, Henry's character was the model of what we like our scientists to be: austere, unselfish, and dedicated. He cared nothing for money or popular applause, except perhaps the approval of a half-dozen fellow physicists who understood his work. To Samuel Morse he had given away the principle of the telegraph with his blessings. Like Benjamin Franklin, he refused to patent a scientific discovery. It was beneath the dignity of science, he insisted. (Though in later years he told a friend with mock ruefulness, "I might have been a little less fastidious.") Indeed, had Henry been more like the Edisons and the Morses, he would have a reputation as one of America's greatest inventors. Unlike them, he was concerned first and foremost with the discovery of new scientific principles. The application, he knew, would follow soon enough from the discovery. That was the way his own inventions had developed. They had come not through laborious trial and error, but directly from his fundamental research into electromagnetism. He left the perfecting of the inventions to others, and he was happy to help as much as he could. This scientific idealism, deepened and strengthened by his Scotch Presbyterian background, was the real secret of Henry's extraordinary prestige

in Washington. Congressmen had rarely met anybody like this stately, somber scientist who knew what he wanted and wanted nothing for himself.

It was Henry who scotched, singlehandedly, Senator Douglas's raid on the Smithsonian's money. Douglas had announced his plan for an agricultural bureau at a farmers' convention that he had shrewdly arranged to hold in the Smithsonian Building. Perhaps Douglas thought the cheering of the farmers would frighten the Smithsonian staff into humble submission. When the cheering stopped, Henry pushed his way to the front of the auditorium and dared to do what many a veteran politician would have feared to undertake: He engaged in a public debate with "the Little Giant" before an audience of the Senator's supporters. Mincing no words, Henry bluntly told the assembled farmers that tampering with the fund dishonored a trust that was both sacred and legal. It would not be done in the name of any group, however worthy. Sharp words passed between Henry and Douglas, but Douglas's raid was stopped in its tracks.

Two years later, in 1854, Henry finally clashed head on with the powerful library faction. In the act establishing the Smithsonian

it was resolved that "the said Regents shall make . . . an appropriation, not exceeding an average of twenty-five thousand dollars annually, for the gradual formation of a library composed of valuable works pertaining to all departments of human knowledge." There were those who felt that the full limit of the $25,000 (all but $5,000 of the annual interest on the bequest) should be spent for a library; indeed, that the Smithsonian should become the Library of Congress.

In the course of the controversy as it was revived in 1854, Henry was forced to dismiss the Smithsonian's librarian. The Board of Regents backed him unreservedly. Dramatically, Rufus Choate resigned from the Board and, in a letter to Congress, charged the Smithsonian with evading the will of the Congress. Congress investigated. Once again the very meaning of Smithson's words was questioned. A letter from Louis Agassiz was read into the *Congressional Record:* ". . . I ought not to omit mentioning a circumstance to which the United States owe the legacy of Smithson, which I happen accidentally to know . . . Smithson had already made his will, and had left his fortune to the Royal Society, when certain scientific papers were offered to that learned body for publication. Notwithstanding his efforts to have them published in their Trans-

actions they were refused, upon which he changed his will. . . ."

After listening to unstinting praise for Henry's policies of research and publication, Congress decided quite firmly that Henry had interpreted the will of Smithson, and the law of Congress, admirably well. For Henry and the Smithsonian it was a great personal vindication. It marked the end of the years of trial. That year—it was 1855—the building was complete, the Smithsonian's policies had been defended in the highest circles, and its freedom of action was assured. With a staff of a half dozen, and an exceptionally small income (as one Congressman exclaimed during the library debate, "Why, a single report of the Patent Office costs three times as much as the entire income of the Smithsonian fund for a year."), the Institution was making itself known in every city of America and Europe. Perhaps the most telling tribute to the work of those early years came not from the learned but from a Brooklyn merchant. In his last will and testament, he left a considerable fortune to the Smithsonian (it was not collected, however, since the bequest was contingent on the death of his children without heirs). "I know of no benevolent institution more useful or appropriate. . . ." It was signed "Thomas Wynn," his mark—X.

The First Secretary
And His "Philosophical Toys"

Electric bell ringer used by Joseph Henry

When Joseph Henry left Princeton to become the first Secretary of the Smithsonian, he brought with him the outlook of a dedicated research scientist. Electromagnetism was his special competence, yet his interests ranged across the entire spectrum of the sciences. On the page opposite, an assemblage of his personal effects, grouped about a youthful portrait, illustrates the far-flung scope of his scientific curiosity—from the battery, bundle of wire, and induction coil that he used to explore the laws of physics, to the notebook, compass, drafting pen, and other tools of the surveyor's trade, which he had practiced as a young man.

Not since Benjamin Franklin had America known a scientific mind of Henry's caliber; and, indeed, his most intensive research took up exactly where Franklin had left off, with the study of electricity. Since Franklin's day American scientists had contributed little to this field, but in Europe one experimenter after another— Galvani, Volta, Oersted, Ampère, names now immortalized in scientific terminology— had piled up an impressive series of discoveries pointing to a close affinity, which Franklin had denied, between magnetic and electrical phenomena. Not the least of these pioneering physicists was François Arago, James Smithson's friend, who in 1820 had demonstrated that a copper wire carrying current affects iron filings the way a magnet does.

With a touch of chauvinism, Henry resolved to revive American interest in electrical investigations, "less generally understood in this country," he observed, "than almost any other department of natural science." In 1825 an Englishman named William Sturgeon had built a magnet with a lifting power of nine pounds by winding eighteen turns of bare copper wire, carrying current, around a varnished bar of soft iron; and with this gadget, the first electromagnet, Henry was fascinated. "Tomorrow I shall make a famous experiment," he told a friend one evening, in 1828, and the next day he made his first important discovery—that by insulating a copper wire (with shreds from his wife's silk petticoat) he could increase the windings about an iron bar without causing a short circuit, and thus increase the magnetic force it produced. Within a year he had built a magnet that could lift fifty times its weight, and soon afterward designed another that, weighing only seventy pounds, could support better than a ton.

Magnets were a mere beginning, though, and Henry rapidly forged ahead. It was a fine thing to produce magnetism from

Henry's most powerful magnet, above, was designed in 1831.

electricity; but, for a nation entering the industrial age, it was a potential revolution to reverse the process, as he saw it, and convert magnetic force into electricity. This dramatic feat, the discovery of electromagnetic induction, Henry performed a full year before Michael Faraday. But, while Faraday took the time to publish his results, and gain credit for the work, Henry was already pressing on. With primitive equipment, he had shown a basic way to produce electric current; now he sought to use that current as a source of mechanical power—in other words, to build a rude electric motor. His small machine, he said, was driven "by a power which I believe has never before been applied in mechanics—by magnetic attraction and repulsion"; and it was strong enough to rock an iron bar, placed upon a pivot, at the rate of seventy-five oscillations per minute. Characteristically, he dismissed it as a mere "philosophical toy," but he also understood its vast potentiality. It is not impossible, he cautiously reported, "that the same principle or some modification of it on a more extended scale may hereafter be applied to some useful purpose."

Usefulness, indeed, was a frequent by-product of Henry's pure research. In 1831, after several trials, he was able to activate an electromagnet at the end of a mile of copper wire stretched about a room—the first electromagnetic telegraph. And one year later he was sending signals across the Princeton campus from his laboratory to his wife at home. Clearly this new device could be exploited to solve the acute communications problem of a country expanding to the west. And Henry, seeing as much, let Samuel Morse take over and adapt his discovery for practical use in a nationwide commercial operation. Unfortunately, out of Henry's act of casual generosity, a bitter quarrel developed. Henry, on the one hand, could not credit Morse with discovering the basic principles of the telegraph, although he did praise him for "bringing it forward at the proper moment" and devising "a plan for carrying it into practical operation." It was an achievement which from a scientific point of view he thought to be of "subordinate importance." Morse, for his part, found Henry's attitude "somewhat queer," and privately observed that the Princeton professor "leaves it for others to do that which alone makes discoveries of any benefit to the world, and strange to say would disparage the man who thus attempts to make scientific discovery beneficial."

This gibe distorted Henry's point. Yet after half a lifetime of original research, Henry was not a man to be seduced by the crass lures of "palpable utility." And this attitude he would stamp upon the Institution. In his tenure as the first Secretary, the precedent was established that the new organization would be guided not by politicians hungry for immediate results, nor by inventive entrepreneurs like Morse, but by men seeking only one reward —in Henry's phrase, "the consciousness of advancing science."

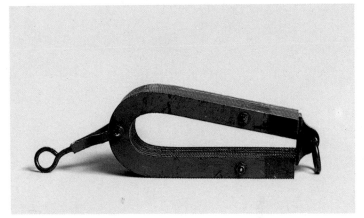

The magnet at right belonged to Professor Henry and is equipped with a "keeper," a device used to confine its lines of force and so conserve its strength. The oscillating model below shows how his first electric motor operated. Another of Henry's motors, above, includes a primitive battery apparatus.

ALL PHOTOGRAPHS BY ARNOLD NEWMAN

KEEL-BILLED TOUCAN
RAMPHASTOS CARINATUS (Swainson)
C.A.

Assembled under a whale skeleton, specimens at left—a huge gorilla, a baboon, an exotic plant, colorful sea creatures and birds, sculptured human heads, a human skeleton and skull—represent only a few of the disciplines pursued by the Smithsonian's Natural History Museum.

PHOTOGRAPH BY ARNOLD NEWMAN

Chapter Two

NATURAL HISTORY

When the Smithsonian Institution was founded, American museums were far from majestic affairs. In 1846 Washingtonians who wanted to see a few oddities could repair to a miscellaneous collection of animal skins and gadgetry crammed into a room at the Patent Office and known, aptly, as the National Cabinet of Curiosities. Philadelphians could lay claim to a more venerable achievement: They had one of the first public museums ever built in America, founded in 1785 by the famous American portrait painter Charles Willson Peale, and conducted as a business enterprise. For a small fee, visitors to Peale's museum could view such disparate delights as the fossil bones of a giant mammoth, a Chinese lady's shoe, and a few pieces of asbestos. Then, in 1813, Charles Willson Peale's son Rembrandt founded a museum in Baltimore where the customers could gaze, as advertised, on "the Grecian Beauty—a Statue in wax from head to foot, colored like Life . . . intended to display the beauty, softness, symmetry, and grace of the female form." That represented the typical American museum in the early nineteenth century: something between a side show and a pawnshop window. The Smithsonian was not even in the running; all it possessed was a collection

of mineral specimens that once belonged to James Smithson.

The few museum owners there were had little to fear even from potential Smithsonian rivalry, for Joseph Henry had a forbidding notion of what a museum should be. It was to be established not primarily for the public's benefit, but for the benefit of science. In Henry's scheme the Smithsonian was going to collect not only what people wanted to see but also what they had no wish to see. As far as the average layman is concerned, if he sees, for example, one bat —preferably the largest—he has seen them all. It is not the same for the natural historian. What he wants, precisely, is to see them all. Bats differ; different kinds live in different locales. They must be named, classified, set in family relation to ancestral bats and to other mammalian forms. A scientist cannot begin to talk about bats or other biological specimens until he classifies them, and he cannot do the fundamental work of classification until he examines his specimens, lined up in a row with their brethren, in study collections. By the middle of the nineteenth century, as Henry saw, the work had barely begun.

Beyond the thirty-one states of the Union stretched the vast and awesome domain of the American West, most of it recently ac-

Pushing toward the Pacific, the ambulance wagon of an early survey party headed by Clarence King makes its way, opposite, across Nevada's Carson Desert in 1867. This vast expanse, the surveyors would recall, was "one of the most desolate and forbidding" that they had crossed. King and his colleagues, with assistance from the Smithsonian, had set out to explore along the fortieth parallel, and—as Henry Adams said—soon "paralleled the Continental Railway in Geology."

Overlooking the Great Divide, a member of another pioneering expedition sets up his gear, above, his bulky cases of equipment piled up at his side. The sights these early naturalists came across were permanently recorded by a generation of wilderness photographers, the greatest of whom was William Henry Jackson, left, whose views of Yellowstone country persuaded Congress to preserve the area as a "public park or pleasuring ground."

quired in several huge pieces. Texas joined the Union in 1845. Most of what are now the states of California, Arizona, Nevada, and Utah—and part of New Mexico—had been acquired from Mexico in 1848. The Oregon and Santa Fe trails had cut across the public domain, and trappers and mountain men had laced pathways through it. Between 1842 and 1849 John C. Frémont, "the Pathfinder," had put sizable stretches of it on crude maps. But as far as scientists were concerned, the West was terra incognita— quite as dark as darkest Africa. Those were the days when half the country believed that "a Great American Desert" lay beyond the one hundredth meridian, while the other half envisioned "a Great American Garden," richer than the Vale of Kashmir, in the Rocky Mountain region. Facts were scarce, but one of Frémont's maps designated a large piece of the West simply as "Sioux Indian War Grounds," and men were not inclined to dawdle there pressing and drying botanical specimens.

When the United States Government was negotiating a boundary with Mexico in 1849, a survey team had to be sent out to determine on which side of the proposed boundary San Diego lay. The expedition returned with specimens of 2,600 plant species no scientist had

seen before. For the research Joseph Henry had in mind, it was apparent that a golden harvest lay to the west—though getting there was going to be difficult.

Fortunately Americans were beginning to move in that direction, and, with the Gold Rush of 1849, the tempo quickened. One traveler who had followed the lonely Oregon Trail in 1848 returned in 1850 to find it littered, relatively speaking, with pots, pans, food, and supplies tossed aside by onrushing prospectors. Indeed, in the 1840's restless Americans were going everywhere. The American consul in Central America disappeared one day in the Guatemalan jungle and emerged as the discoverer of the lost civilization of the Mayas. One naval explorer surveyed the Dead Sea and another sailed up the Amazon River. On his great Expedition to the Pacific Ocean and the South Seas, Lt. Charles Wilkes became, in 1840, the first man to explore the mighty ice sheet of Antarctica. During the pre-Civil War decades, the United States Government was itself leading the way west. Boundaries had to be surveyed, territories established, forts built, and supply routes laid out, or the empire so quickly put together would be in danger of falling as rapidly to pieces. Between 1845 and 1860 some twenty different exploring

A rude campsite in the Yellow-stone was home to the dauntless band of scientists, right, who accompanied Ferdinand V. Hayden on his geological explorations of 1871–1872. For nearly thirty years Professor Hayden ranged across the West, collaborating frequently with the Smithsonian. The varied biological specimens that he sent back, along with ethnological materials, enriched the Institution; and Hayden's naturalists, when they returned, would use Smithsonian facilities to consolidate their findings.

and surveying expeditions were sent out from Washington. Clearly, if the capital were to become the headquarters of exploration, the Smithsonian could become the brain center.

It was ambitious to assume such leadership. In 1850 the Smithsonian's natural history department consisted of only one person, a young naturalist from Reading, Pennsylvania, named Spencer Fullerton Baird. But Baird was superbly equipped for the task; he represented the first of a rising new breed of American naturalists, the sort of men who had sufficient training to meet European standards of excellence. (It was a notable distinction. For an American, a prodigious labor of self-education was necessary to transform just another avid boy collector into a trained and sophisticated biologist.) Perhaps just as importantly, Baird was an enormously winning young man, capable of inspiring deep loyalty and affection in his colleagues, a talent much in demand in an organization with little money. He had been hired by Henry in 1850 as Assistant Secretary of the Smithsonian, charged with responsibility for the small museum. Baird quickly gave it a fresh boost; when he came to Washington he brought along with him an entire freight car full of his own carefully catalogued and classified biological specimens.

Within five years of Baird's arrival, the Smithsonian became the most important biological research center in the country. There was scarcely a Government expedition that did not feel the presence of the Institution in those years. In themselves, the expeditions were severely practical Government enterprises. It was the Smithsonian that insured, in one way or another, that they would have some value for science. Sometimes it was merely necessary to supply expeditions with the required instruments—kettles, sextants, and barometers—needed for systematic field work. Often Baird had to train some young Army officer in the techniques of bird skinning and in such elementary rules of field work as keeping specimens separated according to place of origin. It was rudimentary, of course, but absolutely essential. Without the training, the equipment, and the Smithsonian's handy little field guidebooks, million-dollar expeditions would have returned with little of any worth to scientific research. When scientists today advise the Government on the sorts of instruments to install in the nose cones of rockets, they are doing no more, essentially, than the Smithsonian did over a century ago. The instruments then were barometers, and the rockets teams of army mules, but the exploration of the West was

the space exploration of that day, and equally in need of its scientists. When expeditions returned, Baird and his collaborators wrote official scientific reports for them. Baird was rewarded for his work by the specimens that were brought back to his museum.

Independently of the Government, Baird brought into the Smithsonian's sphere of operations a vast network of ardent volunteers stationed around the country and abroad. Nobody, it seemed, ever left Washington for remote areas without Baird knowing about it. Army surgeons ordered to Western outposts, young diplomatic corpsmen, and simple hobbyists were all set in motion, as Baird remarked, "collecting grist for my mill." Men whose snake collecting had been nothing but a nuisance to their wives discovered that a scientific institution shared their enthusiasm and made scientific sense of their labors. Something of the spirit aroused by the Smithsonian is evident in a letter written to Baird in 1853 by a rural schoolteacher. The note accompanied a sizable box of specimens gathered from fresh-water swamps: "If I *could once* step within [the Smithsonian's] threshold it seems to me my eager eyes and ears and understanding would drink in a world of wonders and knowledge—and that scientific atmosphere! How refreshingly it

would be inhaled . . . while *here* I am compelled to dole out my days and years in anxious and painful ignorance. . . ." It was signed Alexander Winchell, Mesopotamia Female Seminary, Greene County, Alabama.

Other men less wistful than the Alabama schoolteacher did step into "that scientific atmosphere," and stayed on to form the core of the Smithsonian's own small staff of explorers—a community of scholars who pored over their specimens one year and disappeared beyond the one hundredth meridian the next. They had come one by one to the Smithsonian to study under Baird and help with the research. The Institution could not pay them a salary, but it could offer them a place to work; and if they brought their own linen, they could even bed down free in one of the Smithsonian's towers. With youthful, and occasionally boisterous, pride they bore a signal mark of distinction: All of them had been out to the awesome West where men traveled at their peril even under military escort. Today's astronauts could not be any more proudly self-conscious. One Smithsonian crew called itself the Megatherium Club, from the scientific name for a giant fossil sloth. They were high-spirited, somewhat given to shouting Indian war whoops and doing Indian

Dwarfed by Yellowstone's awesome Grand Canyon, the explorers standing at the edge of the chasm above were painted by the adventurer-artist Thomas Moran in 1872.

dances, but there was nothing slothful about them. Indeed, they knew a good deal more of hardship than most men.

The geologist John S. Newberry, for example, wrote home to his Smithsonian friends about the diet of "bread and sand, sand and bacon" that he was enduring on a pioneer expedition through the lunar-like wasteland of Arizona. In 1858 Newberry and a small party of scientists under Lt. Joseph Ives had journeyed west to see if the turbulent Colorado River could be navigated as far as the Mormon country of Utah. The explorers assembled by various routes about sixty miles upstream from the mouth of the Colorado, at Fort Yuma. Within the sand-choked stockade, the garrison was periodically torn apart by mass mutinies and desertions. Outside, the fort was surrounded by outlaw bands and hostile Indians, and a notorious village of sin and rascality known as Colorado City. The explorers put the finishing touches on a homely fifty-four-foot-long paddle-wheel steamer painted bright red. Then, as the soldiers stood by and jeered, Newberry and his cohorts pulled away upstream—and immediately ran aground. The Colorado had given them their first warning. The pilot soon learned the surest mark of danger ahead: Wherever there were hidden shoals, Indians

were clustered, waiting for disaster. The threat of massacre dogged the expedition all the way up the river until, after pushing a few hundred miles upstream, the ship ran aground for the last time. Ives decided that the river was not navigable, and he sent the steamer back. The party continued on foot through the bizarre badlands of western Arizona and, a few weeks later, they were rewarded with one of the most sublime moments of Western exploration: the sight of the immense chasm of the Grand Canyon. At the edge of the cliff, some of the party froze in fear; others, out of some primitive dread, clutched the earth for safety. To a modern tourist, well prepared in advance by hundreds of photographs, the Grand Canyon remains indescribably awesome; to Ives's startled band of explorers, the sight of it threatened to unhinge the mind. Newberry had a chance to study the thousands of feet of exposed rock strata as the expedition made its way down to the canyon floor a mile below the surface of the earth, and he became the first geologist to grasp clearly an important geological truth: that America's Western lands have been largely created by some titanic uplifting of the very crust of the earth. In 1860 it was a concept too grandiose for most scientists to accept, but then no other geologist had seen the Grand

34

Robert Kennicott wears the flamboyant garb of an Arctic explorer in the brooding portrait above. Not long after the picture was taken, the young Smithsonian naturalist died of a heart attack while on an expedition in Alaska.

At the Smithsonian, researchers, above, pore over materials brought back from early expeditions.

Canyon before Newberry. The explorers encountered other surprises as they moved eastward. They discovered a tribe of Hopi Indians living in strange multistoried dwellings seemingly carved out of desert rock. With its cultivated fields and peach trees, the Hopi village looked like the court of Kublai Khan to the exhausted explorers. There, Newberry sat down to write a letter to his friends in Washington. He missed the Smithsonian, he said, and longed for the pleasures he remembered there—the "abundant materials to study, comforting food and clean beds."

A few years later, another Smithsonian protégé, twenty-six-year-old Robert Kennicott, found himself north of the Arctic Circle on Christmas morning in weather forty degrees below zero. Kennicott smoked his last cigar—to the health of "the Megatheria," as he noted in his journal—sang to himself "Do They Miss Me at Home," and set out for a twelve-hour ride by dog sled (his "constitutional," Kennicott said). He was pushing northward, as he had been doing almost steadily for two years. In 1859 he had embarked under Smithsonian auspices on a remarkable one-man collecting expedition to the Canadian wilderness. Starting from Lake Superior, he had worked his way more than a thousand miles northward by boat

and canoe through the chain of lakes and rivers of the Canadian Northwest. His appearance in the north must have been refreshing to the men he encountered. During the decade following his journey, materials poured into the Smithsonian from missionaries and Hudson's Bay Company agents who had not heard of the Smithsonian's work until the genial Kennicott passed through with his guns, nets, and specimen jars.

Kennicott's expeditions to the far north had other important by-products. In 1864 he and a party of Smithsonian scientists were sent out to survey a trail through the almost unknown stretch from the Yukon River to the Bering Strait. Under Joseph Henry's instructions, one of the team, twenty-one-year-old Henry Bannister, was posted to a fort on the Strait to obtain some elementary data on the fabled cold of Russian America, as Alaska was then known.

A work gang of five hundred men trailed the scientists. They had been sent north by the Western Union Company, which hoped to string a telegraph wire to Europe via Alaska and Siberia. When Cyrus Field succeeded in laying a transatlantic cable some years later, Western Union's efforts turned into a three-million-dollar fiasco. The labors of the Smithsonian scientists had better results.

Inside the National Museum Building, opposite, a concrete floor is laid in the 1890's beneath the skeletons of mammals. Completed in 1881, the building was quickly filled with specimens.

Standing in the center of the doorway at left, the Smithsonian's second Secretary, Spencer Baird, checks the progress on construction of the National Museum (now called the Arts and Industries Building). The inspection party includes, from left to right, General M. C. Meigs; General William T. Sherman, Chairman of the Building Committee; Peter Parker, a Regent; Baird; Adolf Cluss, the architect; W. J. Rhees, Chief Clerk; and Daniel Leech, Correspondence Clerk. Above, crowds flock to the completed museum in the 1880's.

In 1867 Henry Bannister returned from the north to Washington —and to the center of a political furor. For a sum of $7,200,000 in gold, the United States Government had just purchased Alaska from the Czar, and the nation's press was pouring out a torrent of abuse. "This territory of ice and snow [is] utterly valueless," ran common editorial opinion. Horace Greeley put it more effectively. Alaska was rich, he said in the New York *Tribune,* "the icefields are inexhaustible and in the burning heat of the Arctic Summer, the Eskimos take refuge in its shade." In that atmosphere of much ridicule and ignorance, the Senate began its debate on ratification of the treaty. Baird and Bannister were asked to testify at a Senate hearing, for outside of the two of them, there was no one in Washington who knew anything about Alaska. They told the committee of the wealth of fisheries, forests, and fur-bearing animals to be found in this so-called territory of ice and snow. Bannister provided the really crucial information on the weather: There was indeed an Arctic summer, and it was surprisingly mild (a fact that had annoyed Bannister in the field, for he had hoped to undergo great hardship). The report did not satisfy the opposition press. According to one newspaper, the Smithsonian's explorers had returned

with tall tales of "an immense lake of molasses and an extensive vale of hasty pudding." But the facts, won at such hard cost, were woven into a powerful three-hour speech by Senator Charles Sumner. It carried the Senate, and Alaska belonged to the United States. In the midst of his second northern expedition, on May 6, 1866, Robert Kennicott died on an Alaskan beach of a heart attack at the age of thirty-one. But his work enabled the Smithsonian to help write an important page of American history.

In the meantime, materials had been accumulating so rapidly at the Smithsonian that the Institution already had the finest collection of natural history specimens in the country. Nonetheless the first step toward establishing a public museum was not taken until 1858 when the National Cabinet of Curiosities, which had been moldering in the Patent Office, was shifted to the Smithsonian's custody. The Cabinet was small compared to the Smithsonian's private collections, but it *was* "national," and with it came a four-thousand-dollar yearly appropriation from Congress. With that start, the Smithsonian turned the main hall of its building into a public museum. A Smithsonian clerk even put out an unofficial pamphlet entitled, somewhat grandly, "Guide to the Smithsonian Institution

and National Museum." The "national museum" was modest enough to fit inside a few large exhibit cases in the present museum's paleontology hall, but it had its admirers. After the Battle of Bull Run, the museum could claim hundreds of daily visitors—convalescing Union troops from nearby Army hospitals.

A few years after the Civil War, the Smithsonian's museum was overflowing with objects. By then it was possible to form separate divisions according to subject matter. The main hall of the building was devoted to the biological sciences, the west wing to geology and fossils, and the large central hall upstairs to a unique collection of American Indian artifacts and costumes. That division was Joseph Henry's particular pride. The study of anthropology, and particularly of the American Indian, had long fascinated the great physicist, in part because it had been so neglected. He had hoped that if the Smithsonian led the way, other organizations and learned societies would join in, and the Smithsonian would then be free to find new subjects for study. It was always Henry's policy to get as much research started as possible (frequently turning over the follow-up work to another); but the study of the American Indian had a special urgency. Before the work had begun, the very sub-

ject matter—the Indians themselves—was perishing. Already, whole tribes like the Mandan had been wiped out by disease, unrecorded and largely unlamented. Others had been reduced by contact with whites to the pitiful level of army-post scavengers. The Smithsonian had started work as early as 1847. It had published in its various reports some of the best pioneer research in anthropology. The very first Smithsonian publication, in fact, had been a classic study of Mississippi Valley Indian mounds, the evidence of an earlier people who mysteriously had died out in America. The Smithsonian sent out circulars and questionnaires asking for information about Indians. One questionnaire was drawn up by Charles Darwin. He was eager for information about the facial mannerisms of primitive peoples, such as: "Is the head nodded vertically in affirmation and shaken laterally in negation?" Darwin asked that the observations be made on tribes who had had little contact with Europeans. But Henry's problem was precisely that too many Indians had been influenced by white men; those who had not been were hidden deep in the Rockies or the almost uninhabitable Western deserts. Few men cared to explore the Rockies, and the men who did venture there took pains to avoid the Indians. It was clear that what

This fifteenth-century wooden deer's head, carved by a Calusa Indian, is a fine example of prehistoric art found at Key Marco, Florida. Employed in ceremonies, it may also have been used as a decoy for game. The movable ears were manipulated by strings. George Catlin, the great Western artist, gave the colorful woven quillwork band (below) to the Smithsonian Institution.

Collections at the Smithsonian include recordings in many Indian tongues. An Indian woman, with two fellow tribesmen, talks into a dictating machine, above.

the Smithsonian needed was an altogether new kind of explorer.

In the spring of 1867, just such a man came to Henry. He was a thirty-five-year-old former Army major from Illinois, with a bushy beard and rumpled clothes. One of his arms had been shot off at the Battle of Shiloh. His name was John Wesley Powell (see p. 40), and he had come to borrow some scientific instruments for a geological exploration of the Rocky Mountains of the Colorado. There was one uncharted spot left on the map of the United States, and Powell, the self-taught geologist, was drawn to it as to a magnet. The unknown territory was a piece of land five hundred miles long and two hundred miles wide through which the Colorado ran much of its course. The terrors of the Colorado were widely celebrated in mountaineers' stories: Steep walls rose directly up from the river's edge for two miles; they would pin a boatman in a death-trap of giant sucking whirlpools and steep waterfalls to match Niagara. The one-armed major ignored the mountaineers and decided to risk a trip through what he would later call "the Great Unknown." On May 24, 1869, Powell and eight crewmen pushed off in four small boats down a Wyoming tributary of the river.

It was to be the last great exploration on American soil. Three months later, half-starved and half-naked, beaten by the churning waters, and nerves raw from the incessant roar of the river, Powell and six remaining crewmen had worked their way nine hundred miles downstream on the other side of the Grand Canyon. The Colorado was conquered, and Powell was a national hero.

On this first exploration of the Colorado region, Powell came upon the shy, still unspoiled Ute and Shoshoni Indians. Camping among them one winter, he persuaded a chieftain to tell him some of the myths and legends of his people. As he listened, it seemed to Powell that he was hearing not simply an old man's tribal lore, but a surviving relic of what human thought must have been in man's primeval, mythmaking past. Among the primitive peoples, he came to believe that he could trace the very beginnings of the spiritual evolution of man.

Ultimately, in 1879, Congress formally placed Powell's researches under the care of the Smithsonian and gave him a twenty-thousand-dollar appropriation for his work. Powell turned the money into one of the most vigorous divisions of the Smithsonian Institution, the Bureau of American Ethnology, which did more to salvage the languages, legends, and customs of the American Indian than did

CONTINUED ON PAGE 43

John Wesley Powell: Founding the B.A.E.

When John Wesley Powell was only thirteen, a large band of Winnebago Indians suddenly set up camp on his family's farm in southern Wisconsin. By day they fished and hunted; at night they grouped around their fires to sing, dance, and recite their ancient tribal legends. And when at last they departed, young Powell was left with an unforgettable memory of their fascinating ways. Years later, after many more encounters with the Indians on his far-flung geological explorations Major Powell, opposite, in conversation with a Paiute chief, was ready to convert his boyhood enthusiasm into a mature, scientific program. Armed with a grand scheme to "organize anthropologic research in America," he began in 1879 to build his Bureau of American Ethnology, the famous B.A.E.

It was a task of formidable dimensions to investigate the scattered peoples who had roamed America before the white man, and Powell found little precedent to guide him. Anthropology, the science of man, was terra incognita in America at the time; and though Powell himself had once taught a solitary course on prehistoric man at Illinois Wesleyan University, not a single college in the country offered regular instruction in the field. Indeed, the only diligent students of the first Americans were not the Americans themselves, but agents sent out by European governments, led by France, to ship back tons of relics for firsthand scrutiny by Continental scholars.

Unfortunately, Powell could not successfully transplant the science of these European savants to American soil. Their traditional method was to classify different racial types according to their physical characteristics. But Powell was out to solve another kind of problem. The decade of the 1880's was a time of bitter tragedy for the American Indian, as the fierce Apache warrior Geronimo spread savage havoc in a last futile effort to save his people's way of life. Saddened by the misfortune of the Indians, Powell formed a humanitarian plan to group together different tribes on common reservations of good, tillable land. Yet all too obviously some Indian groups could not be combined harmoniously. It was the major's observation that tribes with similar traditions would live together peaceably, while those whose cultures differed were likely to become irreconcilable enemies. And so, motivated by a pressing public need, he chose to pioneer in the novel science of ethnology, a branch of anthropology that seeks to classify the rich variety of mankind not by physical but by cultural distinctions.

From his tiny office in the Smithsonian, Powell directed a massive, almost military, campaign to comprehend what he termed the Indian humanities. Weapons and tools, jewelry and paintings, myths and vocabularies—all were data for his inquiry. And within a decade, with the rigor of his early training as a naturalist, he had reduced more than eight hundred Indian tribes to fifty-nine linguistic stocks, each with roughly uniform cultural patterns.

Such systematic labor was Powell's distinctive genius, and he always viewed the studies undertaken by his bureau as similar in method to the other branches of natural history. Once, in conference with a group of Shivwit Indians, he attempted to explain the purpose of his travels. The greatest white man, he told them in his best Paiute, "is he who knows the most . . . about the mountains and the valleys, the rivers and the canyons, the beasts and birds and snakes." To this wondrous list of natural phenomena, Powell simply added the Indians themselves. For all were bound together in his mind into a single scientific enterprise, man and nature being one. Guided by this unifying vision, the major built a monument that would live beyond him, a bureau renowned throughout the entire learned world for its pathfinding research in American ethnology.

Secretary Langley breaks ground in 1904, above, for the Smithsonian's Museum of Natural History. At right, with its four stories comprising more than ten acres, the building nears completion as massive granite slabs are hoisted up the side of the structure that faces the Mall. Below, a street market flourishes on the cobblestone street on the north side of the building as it was in 1909. The museum was not finished until 1911.

Kermit and Theodore Roosevelt pose at right with antelopes bagged during their African safari in 1909. Dubbed "Bwana Tumbo" (Mr. Portly Man) by the Swahili, "T.R." posed, too, with jaguars, lions, a stork, a bull rhinoceros, and a goodly number of other animals—all shipped back to the Smithsonian. The safari was only one, though perhaps the most famous, of many expeditions that brought back specimens for the Museum of Natural History.

CONTINUED FROM PAGE 39

any other group in the country. Recently the bureau has been merged into the Smithsonian Office of Anthropology, but the work of salvaging the record of Indian life continues. Since 1945 the Smithsonian River Basin Surveys have been locating and recovering the precious remains of prehistoric Indian life. The River Basin project, too, has been working against time, trying to complete the research before dams back up the waters of America's rivers and bury forever the ethnologists' treasures.

The Bureau of American Ethnology was not the first research project to be supported by the Government for the Smithsonian. In 1871 Spencer Baird had been asked to head a temporary commission to investigate the disastrous decline of Atlantic food fish. Establishing himself at Woods Hole, Massachusetts, Baird quickly found the reason: Commercial fishermen were catching the fish before they could reach their spawning grounds. Since there was no legal way to stop the fishermen, the only recourse was to increase the supply of fish. Under the auspices of the Smithsonian, the Fish Commission began its work of developing rich sources of food where none previously existed. Fish hatcheries were created; carp were introduced into twenty thousand streams throughout Ameri-

ca; and shad were transferred to the Pacific coast, where they now thrive. Eventually Baird's Fish Commission grew into the United States Bureau of Fisheries—another Smithsonian seedling that has far outgrown the parent in size.

The Institution's labors on the nation's behalf did not go unrewarded. Though it had been created largely through a private trust, the Smithsonian's museum had become national in all but name. On May 13, 1878, Joseph Henry died, in his eighty-first year, and memorial services were held for him in the Capitol. In the following year Congress formally recognized the museum's status. That year, a quarter of a million dollars was appropriated by Congress to build a second Smithsonian building to be known as the National Museum. In addition Congress stipulated that all specimens of scientific value collected by any Government agency were to be deposited in the National Museum under Smithsonian custody. What previously had been earned by hard barter and hard work was now to come in automatically. Within fifteen years after the red-brick new building was completed, it was already overcrowded; and in 1911 a monumental new $3,500,000 home was built across the Mall for the use of the Museum of Natural History.

Established under the Smithsonian in 1946, the headquarters of the Canal Zone Biological Area, above, is set in a lush tropical forest where the annual rainfall mounts to one hundred inches. More than fifty scientists and students brave its climate each year for biological studies.

By then there was no longer any need to cajole a donor. It had become an honor—even for presidents—to aid in the work of the natural history museum. When Teddy Roosevelt set off on his famed African safari in 1909, he went as a Smithsonian volunteer, with a long list of targets drawn up for him by the museum staff. "I am not in the least a game butcher," Roosevelt insisted, and he was proud to be able to claim that he had killed only the animals the Institution had asked for. Roosevelt returned with the skins of fifty-four different kinds of large mammals, including lions, elands, and elephants, many of which are still on display at the museum. Following Roosevelt other hunters brought back their trophies to what had become "the venerable Smithsonian," solidly planted on the Mall in three fine buildings.

Today, of course, the American frontier is gone, and Government exploring parties no longer drive mules through unknown native lands. But explorations continue to embark from the Smithsonian, and newly discovered forms of life are still being brought back to the Institution. In 1964, for example, Smithsonian anthropologists were living among a near-extinct Brazilian tribe, an archaeologist was excavating in Mexico, a Smithsonian marine biologist was cruising the Indian Ocean, and a botanist was on an expedition in Africa—to name but a few projects. The collections in various branches of natural history have by now grown spectacularly large. The Department of Botany has a collection of well over 3,000,000 plants, which constitutes what is known as the National Herbarium. The Department of Zoology's Division of Mammals has over 300,000 skins in its archives. The Division of Birds has 500,000 birds representing most of the world's one thousand species. The Department of Mineral Sciences has some 90,000 specimens including most of the 1,800 kinds of minerals in the world. The Office of Anthropology has nearly 1,000,000 specimens in addition to the largest archives of photographs and manuscripts concerning the archaeology, ethnology, languages, and history of the American Indian north of Mexico. The Department of Paleobiology's research collections include more than 13,000,000 specimens of fossil plants and animals. The Department of Entomology has over 16,000,000 insects. The Smithsonian has one biological archive too large to fit in any building: the entire island of Barro Colorado in the Canal Zone, where a tropical rain forest is preserved in its pristine state for scholars—one of few tropical research outposts

River Basin Survey archaeologists, above, work quickly to retrieve the remains of prehistoric Indians from an ancient house floor along the crumbling banks of the Missouri River. Salvaging materials before dams back up the waters of the Missouri, the teams send their finds back to the Smithsonian for analysis. At left, near the Fort Randall Reservoir in South Dakota, a Survey crew unearths a mass of skeletons from an Indian burial pit.

in the Americas that is available to scientists. The island is set in the midst of Gatun Lake, which, in turn, is surrounded by montane forests, marsh, savanna, and mangrove forests so dense, it is said, that fireflies light up in the daytime. The area is populated by monkeys, all the characteristic groups of Neotropical birds, iguanas, jaguars, anteaters—and a myriad of insects. This 3,600-acre "specimen" is known as the Canal Zone Biological Area.

Most of this vast assemblage the public will never see. It forms an almost unparalleled collection of natural history. The familiar analogy of the iceberg comes to mind, for the Smithsonian that the public sees is but a fraction of the great bulk of material the Institution has. Perhaps a more useful comparison would be that of a library, which has a few books on the open shelves for circulation and thousands upon thousands more which only scholars employ; for the study collections of the Smithsonian are consulted quite as if they were books in a library. During World War II, for example, the Japanese launched incendiary bombs across the Pacific. When one landed unexploded on the West Coast, investigators discovered specks of sand still adhering to the bomb. They were sent to the Smithsonian, where, with the help of a

study collection, the exact source of the sand was determined and the launching area pinpointed for American bombers. Oil companies frequently consult what is the most insignificant-looking collection in the entire natural history museum—tiny fossils of marine protozoa no bigger than bits of sand. Each speck is kept in a neat little box as though it were a crown jewel. To the oil companies the fossils are crucially important. The kind of foraminifer dredged up by an oil rig indicates the geological age of the rock strata from which the oil was pumped. With the information obtained from these specimens oil companies can map out a wide adjacent area of possible oil-bearing strata. The Entomology Department applies its collection to a vital but little-known fight to keep insect pests from entering the country. When a customs official discovers some odd insect lurking in, for example, a banana shipment from Central America, the insect is sent to the Smithsonian for identification as a matter of routine. If it turns out to be a pest, all shipments from the country of origin may be stopped. Recently an amateur collector discovered an unusual scarab beetle in New Jersey and asked the Smithsonian to identify it. It turned out to be a European insect pest that had somehow come into the port of New

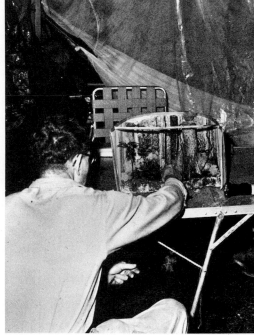

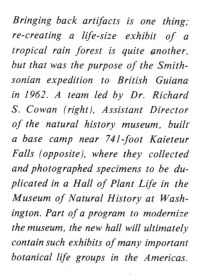

Bringing back artifacts is one thing; re-creating a life-size exhibit of a tropical rain forest is quite another, but that was the purpose of the Smithsonian expedition to British Guiana in 1962. A team led by Dr. Richard S. Cowan (right), Assistant Director of the natural history museum, built a base camp near 741-foot Kaieteur Falls (opposite), where they collected and photographed specimens to be duplicated in a Hall of Plant Life in the Museum of Natural History at Washington. Part of a program to modernize the museum, the new hall will ultimately contain such exhibits of many important botanical life groups in the Americas.

At the camp, above, an artist works on a scale model of the exhibit. Certain plants and vines, collected by teams like the one seen at top left, are shipped to the Smithsonian; huge trees will be modeled after photographs and rubber molds. Thomas Soderstrom, a staff botanist and photographer, took these pictures as part of his work.

York. Knowing what happened when the notorious Japanese beetle slipped into New Jersey many years ago, the Smithsonian alerted the Government to watch for signs of its spread.

Examples of such practical uses of the Smithsonian's study collections can be multiplied at length. But their importance ought not to be misunderstood. The Smithsonian's collections were not put together for an immediate practical use; they are of practical use because they have been put together with the natural historian's need for completeness. Because the book of nature is far from complete, the Smithsonian continues its work of collection and classification. Botanists at the Smithsonian estimate that 70 per cent of the plant life of South America is still unknown to science. Entomologists are in an even more critical situation: They face what amounts to a biological avalanche. There may be as many as three million different insect species in the world; of that number some two million are still unaccounted for. Not long ago a boy brought to the curators an entirely new species of what had been considered a particularly well-known insect genus. He had found it a few miles from the Smithsonian. The Smithsonian's paleontologists still continue to explore the world for fossils, for the scheme of evolution charted by Charles Darwin over a century ago still has far more missing links than reliable evidence. Last year a Smithsonian paleontologist was able to provide one of the links. In the Karroo region of South Africa, he discovered huge fossil skulls of mammal-like reptiles, typical of a group of extinct creatures that represent a stage in the evolutionary development of the mammal (and man) from its reptilian ancestors.

In a few fields of natural history the record is fairly complete. It is unlikely, for example, that anyone will discover any large number of new bird species to be classified. So Smithsonian ornithologists are free to explore other kinds of biological problems, such as the complex relationship between animals and their environments. The Smithsonian staff has chosen for study a 4,500,000-square-mile area of the central Pacific. There the team has banded 450,000 birds of about one hundred different species in order to keep track of their distribution, nesting, eating, and flying habits in relation to temperatures, ocean currents, marine life, and other factors. Even in this type of study, the earlier work in classification has proven essential. Ornithologists can take for granted that the birds they are studying are adequately classified, that oceanograph-

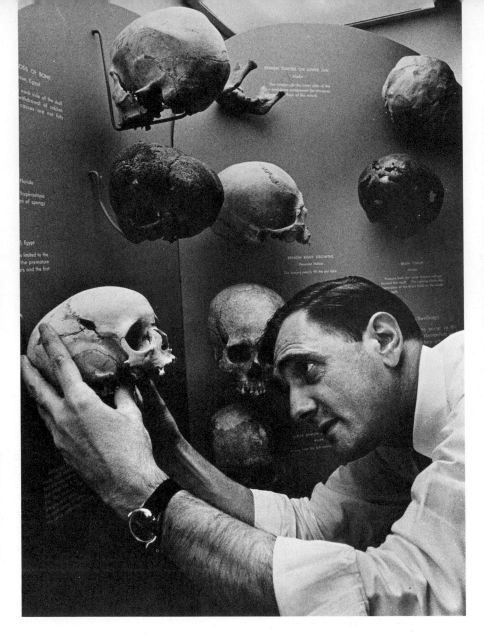

Minute bits of bones are analyzed and classified below by a Smithsonian researcher. Some of the best-preserved specimens are eventually put on display, and, recently, the Museum of Natural History has rejuvenated old display cases with freshly designed "story" exhibits. At right, a skull is placed in a case showing how some diseases of prehistoric man are diagnosed from skeletons.

BOTH PHOTOGRAPHS BY ARNOLD NEWMAN

ers have charted the central Pacific currents, and that marine biologists have collected enough specimens from this region of the Pacific so that the investigators can say more about the feeding habits of the birds under study than that they eat fish.

The great natural history archives have been established and catalogued, not for any particular reason, but for the most general possible reason: to be there when called upon, for there is no telling when a new departure in scientific inquiry will require the archives. Fashions in science change, but the Smithsonian's work is not prey to fads. For many years Smithsonian curators went to considerable lengths to add new meteorites to their collection. In June, 1938, for example, a Smithsonian curator read in the newspaper that a meteorite had passed over Pittsburgh and frightened the populace. Where the meteorite landed, nobody knew. The Smithsonian went quickly into action: In Pittsburgh hundreds of people who had seen the missile in flight were interviewed and asked to trace out what they thought the trajectory had been. Combining all the estimates on a map, curators pinpointed the little hamlet of Chicora, Pennsylvania. They rushed there to discover the meteorite nestling in a farmer's chicken yard. Of the two thou-

sand known meteorites in the world, the Smithsonian has specimens of some twelve hundred—the finest collection in the world. Today, research in meteorites has become quite fashionable, along with all other kinds of space research, and today the Smithsonian is one of the world's centers for that work.

Here the analogy with the library breaks down badly, for the Smithsonian's Museum of Natural History is a library of a peculiar type. Its books are written in a kind of hieroglyphics which the curator must decipher to make his collections of use. The hieroglyphics of meteorites are especially compelling, for meteorites are the only specimens from outer space man has ever possessed. They represent something like primordial matter—random pieces of the universe. Yet in puzzling ways meteorites differ from similar chunks of stone and iron found on the earth. Every difference is a clue to a fact about outer space. When iron meteorites are sliced by machines, their silvery metallic surfaces reveal a great variety of lacy patterns not found in terrestrial iron—those too are hieroglyphics. Recently a Smithsonian investigator noticed a tiny speck of glass embedded in a piece of meteorite he was examining under a microscope. What intrigued him was that whereas glass

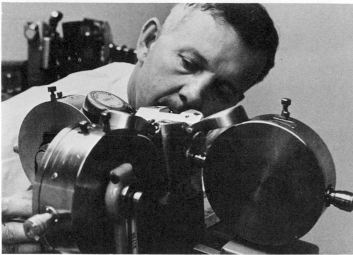

In a section of the electron microprobe laboratory, above, a mineralogist examines a meteorite taken from the comprehensive Smithsonian collection.

Meteorites, resembling nothing so much as unprepossessing rocks, like the one above, yield unexpected new information when analyzed. A greatly magnified segment of the stony Chainpur meteorite at right reveals glassy chondrules.

known on earth disintegrates in a few thousand years, this meteoritic glass had been produced by conditions that enabled it to last about four billion years. Such meteorites have provided some hotly debated new theories. In another, quite separate branch of the Smithsonian Institution known as the Astrophysical Observatory, the study of metcoritics has been pursued to such an extent that the observatory has taken a place at the center of some of the most fundamental, and arresting, controversies of modern science. The director of the observatory, Dr. Fred L. Whipple, has worked out what he calls "the Cold Theory"—a hypothesis that may overturn all scientists' previous notions on the origin of the universe. Another researcher maintains that the glassy chondrules found in a number of meteorites are actually the first solid particles of the solar system. Still others are analyzing meteorites to see whether they contain evidence of life in outer space.

The study of meteorites is a long way from the earth-bound spheres of natural history, yet this new work was begun with the motive that has always inspired the Smithsonian's natural historians: the desire to give a faithful account and keep a complete record of all that man can know about the natural life around him.

A Living Museum

Grazing in a back-yard pen of the Smithsonian, above, two forlorn specimens of the vanishing American buffalo pose for a photographer in the late 1880's.

There is one Smithsonian museum where the exhibits are alive, noisy, and sometimes dangerous. Kept behind iron bars and fences, nearly three thousand animals now inhabit the National Zoological Park, located on a wooded tract of land just twenty minutes by car from the Mall; and four million visitors a year stroll through its shady grounds. There they may come across a rare white tigress with her cubs (one of which is also white), pigmy hippopotamuses, or the black-faced ibis at right, a proud new resident of the zoo's latest and most spectacular addition, the handsome remodeled birdhouse that was opened to the public in 1965.

The Smithsonian's zoo was founded seventy-five years ago by Samuel Pierpont Langley, a middle-aged astrophysicist who had a bachelor's fondness for entertaining children. In 1887, when Langley became the third Secretary of the Institution, some two hundred assorted creatures, huddled together in sheds behind the old Smithsonian Building, constituted a miscellaneous menagerie that the National Museum had assembled to serve as taxidermists' models. When their modeling days were over, these living specimens were either killed to obtain their skins and skeletons, or shipped off to retirement at the Philadelphia Zoo. But even while only temporarily detained in Washington, they had become a popular side show for the crowds that swarmed about the Smithsonian museums on Sunday afternoons.

Among the species quartered by the Insitution were six buffaloes, survivors of the fifty million that once had roamed over the American continent. Less than a thousand of their kind still remained, and Secretary Langley took it upon himself to provide these beasts with "places of seclusion in which to breed, and replenish their dying race. . . ." On April 30, 1890, Congress formally established the National Zoo, "for the advancement of science and the instruction and recreation of the people." And soon afterward, the Smithsonian's back-yard zoo was carted five miles northwest, under the watchful eye of a former Barnum and Bailey circus man, William H. Blackburn, to a 175-acre site in the Rock Creek area, where a single, inexpensive animal house had been hastily constructed to see them through the winter.

Since then, despite a slender budget, the National Zoo has missed few opportunities to add exotic creatures to its collections. Once, during an especially lean year, a traveling animal show arranged to camp for the winter season in Rock Creek valley by agreeing to

Above, a denizen of the monkey house ponders visitors.

The Komodo dragon above was given to the zoo by Indonesia's President Sukarno.

give the zoo, in partial payment of the rent, one half the number of animals that would be born during the visit. Though the returns from this speculative venture amounted to only two kangaroos and a lion, other animals were already arriving in increasing numbers. Ever since the Abyssinian Emperor Menelik II gave Teddy Roosevelt two baboons, a zebra, a lion, and an ostrich, which the President promptly sent to the zoo, the animal collection has benefited dramatically by gifts from foreign potentates. Recent acquisitions include a pair of Dorcas gazelles from Tunisia's President Habib Bourguiba and two Komodo dragons from Indonesia's Sukarno. Special expeditions, too, have brought back creatures to enrich the variety of the Zoological Park. One exploring party, financed by Walter P. Chrysler, and led by the zoo's famous director W. M. Mann, returned from Africa in 1926 with a shipload of giraffes, leopards, hyenas, and other wild beasts that, in a single stroke, nearly doubled the census at the zoo. And when Admiral Byrd visited Antarctica, a representative of the zoo went with him to gather penguins and send them back to Washington.

Just feeding the small community of animals nestled in the Rock Creek valley has become an arduous exercise in logistics, and every year the dieticians of the National Zoo purchase some two hundred tons of hay, seventy tons of crushed oats, and thirty tons of corn to satisfy the enormous appetites of their charges. Though visitors often try to supplement this diet, the results have not always been satisfactory. Some years ago, when a six-thousand-pound river hippopotamus named Bongo died, an autopsy revealed in his stomach a plastic wallet, one hundred pennies, a lipstick case, several pounds of sand and rocks, a quantity of marbles, some subway tokens, a .22-caliber cartridge case, and other indigestible items that thoughtless admirers had thrown him for amusement.

Not all that happens at the zoo, of course, is calculated to amuse the public. Artists and naturalists frequently use the facilities to study animals, and present plans call for a vigorous expansion of this scientific program. For if a national zoo seems a curious place to advance the frontiers of human knowledge, there is always the example of Secretary Langley himself hovering in the background. It was at the zoo that he observed and photographed the flight of vultures and other birds, from a special platform built into an oak tree; and this research played a crucial part in his pioneering efforts to build a machine capable of flight.

"Willie," the coy hybrid bear above, begs peanuts from friendly tourists.

"Mohini," the rare white tigress above, gave birth in 1964 to the first white tiger ever born and bred outside India.

A hippopotamus (right) basks in the sun beside her baby, which at birth weighed seventy pounds.

Two of the Smithsonian's early contributions to the study of flight are shown here: Samuel Langley's Aerodrome Six, *to the left of Alan Shepard's* Mercury *capsule; and Dr. Robert Goddard's first successful rocket, at upper left. Alongside the red brick Arts and Industries Building loom monsters of the modern U.S. space program.*

PHOTOGRAPH BY ARNOLD NEWMAN

Chapter Three

FLIGHT, SPACE, AND THE ELEMENTS

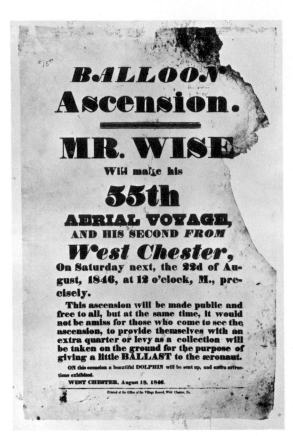

Joseph Henry often took advantage of opportunity where he found it. The poster above promoted the activities of John Wise, who carried some of Henry's instruments aloft. Another balloonist befriended by the Smithsonian's first Secretary was Thaddeus S. C. Lowe, shown at right in the starred and striped gondola of the balloon Intrepid, *rising above Union Army tents in Virginia. For two years during the Civil War, Lowe and his aerial observers floated over the battlefields, spotting the Confederate movements.*

The Smithsonian studies more than one genus of natural history, if the physical sciences may be called such. While Kennicott, Baird, Powell, and their colleagues were scattered over the earth searching for clues to the history of man and his planet, another group of scientists began to search the sky, and space, for an understanding of other, at first glance less tangible, laws of nature.

Compared with the reaches of space now probed by researchers at the Smithsonian Astrophysical Observatory, for example, the Institution began its work fairly close to the ground, with the weather, which in 1846 had finally become something worth talking about. In the hands of a few pioneer American meteorologists, a new idea was taking shape in the decade of the 1840's. The weather, these men were discovering, was not simply a local caprice. The storm that hit Cape Hatteras one day and the storm that struck Boston a few days later were very likely to be the same disturbance—a spiraling swirl of air, subject to natural laws, that traveled along the great currents of the aerial ocean the way little whirlpools might travel along the current of a river. A new branch of science—the tracking of storms—had suddenly opened up, and the Smithsonian wasted no time in taking up the work. It was an ex-

Abraham Lincoln was painted (below) with the founders of the National Academy of Sciences by the artist Albert Herter. From left to right are: Benjamin Peirce, an astronomer; Alexander Dallas Bache, a physicist, Regent of the Smithsonian, and first president of the National Academy of Sciences; Joseph Henry; the naturalist Louis Agassiz; Lincoln; Senator Henry Wilson, a member of the Senate military affairs committee during the Civil War; Admiral Charles Davis, a naval commander during the Civil War; and Benjamin Apthorp Gould, the founder of the Astronomical Journal. *Lincoln, with an avid amateur's interest in science, patented a device for lifting ships off sand bars, and spent many hours in a tower of the Smithsonian Building during the Civil War, talking with Joseph Henry and watching the Secretary conduct his experiments.*

citing prospect, for with the work of the Smithsonian, scientific weather forecasting was born.

Helped by Congressmen who canvassed their districts for likely candidates, the Smithsonian by 1848 had organized a corps of one hundred and fifty amateur weather observers around the country as part of a two-pronged attack on what Henry called the problem of American storms. Then, to outrace the storms thus charted, Henry persuaded telegraph companies to submit an account every morning of the weather conditions at the various telegraph stations. By that simple expedient, the world's first telegraphic weather service was formed as a private operation of the Smithsonian Institution. By co-ordinating the reports from his observers. Henry was able to make up what was possibly the most valuable single tool in meteorology: America's first current weather map. With it, Henry could venture, cautiously at least, to predict the weather, and soon the Smithsonian's tower was signaling storm warnings to coastal authorities. In 1857 the Washington *Evening Star* stole a march on the world's newspapers and began publishing daily the Smithsonian's comprehensive weather reports, which replaced the local weather notices that had been faithfully sent in each week by a cer-

tain "B. of Georgetown." And, eventually, the success of the Smithsonian's weather department resulted in the founding of the United States Weather Bureau by Congress.

The Smithsonian's weather researches led to some curious, and productive, byways. For some years Joseph Henry extracted meteorological information from John Wise, one of America's foremost balloonists. Wise had an unbounded faith in the usefulness of balloons—strengthened no doubt when one of his balloons burst two miles up in the air, only to form a parachute and bring Wise down to the ground unhurt. At one time he ventured aloft for the Smithsonian in the midst of an electrical storm. He dubbed his research balloon *The Smithsonian,* and his ascent through lightning into a cloud helped buttress the Institution's researches in atmospheric electricity.

Informed by such experiments with balloons, Henry later had some dealings with "Professor" Thaddeus S. C. Lowe of New Hampshire, self-styled scientist, showman, and builder of an exceedingly large balloon intended for a flight across the Atlantic Ocean. In 1860 Lowe's backers wrote to the Smithsonian for scientific approval of his transoceanic flight. Henry replied that the

voyage was feasible, but he suggested that Lowe first try a more modest experimental flight over land. On April 20, 1861, Lowe took off in a smaller balloon from Cincinnati. It was a truly splendid flight. As he crossed the Appalachians, Lowe was four miles up and speeding along in his open basket at one hundred miles an hour. When he sighted the Atlantic Ocean in the distance, Lowe began to deflate the balloon, and gently floated to earth, where he was arrested on the spot by South Carolina authorities as a Union spy. The Civil War had just broken out.

When Lowe, pleading a purely scientific curiosity, finally extricated himself from the Confederacy, he hurried to Washington and offered to form a balloon corps for the Northern Army, but General Winfield Scott refused to listen. Disappointed, he turned to Henry who brought his new protégé to see the President of the United States. Together they strenuously urged Abraham Lincoln to consider the idea. Under Henry's direction a trial was made of Lowe's balloon near the Smithsonian grounds. As he hovered above the capital with a telegraph wire strung from his basket, Lowe sent the President the first aerial telegram in history: "Sir . . . the city with its girdle of encampment presents a superb view." It took

some further persuasion on Henry's part to overcome the massive indifference of the military, but he finally won recognition for Lowe. Boasting several observation balloons and the dauntless professor, the Union's Aeronautics Corps defied knife-wielding saboteurs and irate Southern gunners for two years at the front. It was the first military air arm in American history.

By the time of the Civil War another intriguing device vied with weather maps and balloons for the attention of physical scientists. Chemists had created the spectroscope, an instrument capable of analyzing the chemical nature of any substance whose light was submitted to it, whether the substance was in the same room or millions of miles distant. And with the spectroscope, one more new science was born: astrophysics, the study of the physical constitution of heavenly bodies. As early as 1870 Joseph Henry urged the construction of an observatory devoted to the new field. Failing in that, in 1887 the nation's leading astrophysicist, Samuel Pierpont Langley (see p. 62), was brought in as an Assistant Secretary.

Working since 1867 at the Allegheny Observatory in Pennsylvania, Langley had made outstanding advances in man's knowledge of the sun and its radiation. His greatest contribution was the

Aerodrome Five, *photographed at left by Alexander Graham Bell as it took off over the Potomac on May 6, 1896, was Secretary Langley's first successful unmanned flying machine. "His demonstration," Wilbur Wright said some years later, "had great influence in determining my brother and myself to take up work in this science. . . ." In 1899, Wilbur wrote to the Smithsonian (below) requesting literature about the problems of flight, and received in reply a bundle of pamphlets that helped the two brothers to refine their experiments.*

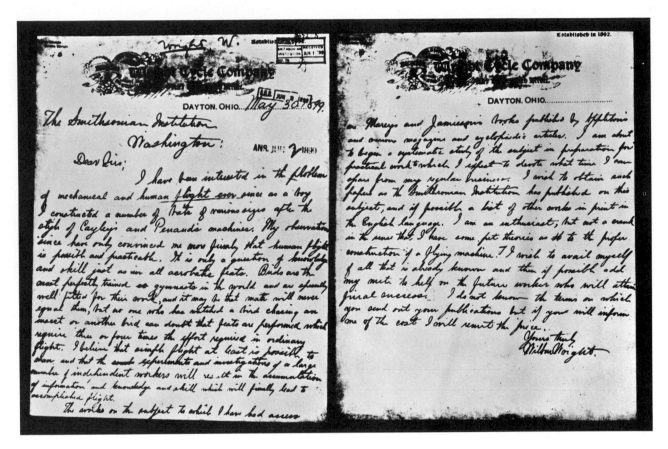

refinement of a device known as the bolometer, which he said was capable of detecting temperature changes of as little as one ten-millionth of a degree centigrade. By means of this device, Langley was able to determine the heat of the sun and the reflected energy of the moon, and calculate the heat-absorbing characteristics of the atmosphere. Most importantly, he was able to discover a portion of the infrared spectrum of the sun's radiation, a momentous revelation to astrophysicists.

A resolute believer in the worth and possibilities of the "new astronomy," as he liked to call astrophysics, Langley profoundly influenced the course of research at the Smithsonian when, after the death of Spencer Baird in 1887, he became its third Secretary. He brought with him an unusual research project—the study of solar radiation as a key to the world's weather—and in 1890 he created an organization to carry out the work: the Smithsonian Astrophysical Observatory. It was the nation's first observatory exclusively devoted to the "new astronomy." In 1895 it consisted of two sheds on the Smithsonian grounds (built with the help of a five-thousand-dollar gift from Langley's friend Alexander Graham Bell) with grass growing uncut around them. As an assistant of

Langley's remarked at the time, "[He] keeps the grass long so that news writers will not think there is anybody there."

In the meantime, Langley took up still another field that called for daring innovation. At the age of fifty-three, in the year he became Secretary of the Smithsonian, he placed himself and the Institution in the center of what was for him an entirely new field: the study of heavier-than-air flight. That he ventured into the field at all was remarkable in itself. Many scientists had long since washed their hands of the subject. Man would never fly, according to most scientists; the example of the birds was simply a delusion.

There was nothing sensational, however, about Langley's opening attack on the problem. He proposed to investigate in a methodical way a principle that had been toyed with intermittently for centuries—that inclined surfaces moving through the air receive a "lift." Whether it was enough to make the flight of man-made aircraft possible was the question to which Langley addressed himself. For three years he attempted to measure the lift produced on inclined planes placed at the end of a rapidly rotating thirty-foot-long arm, and his results provided a much-needed ray of hope for the aeronautical dreamers: "Mechanical flight," announced

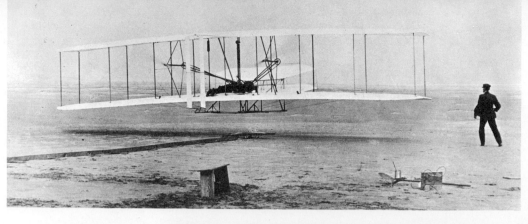

Just nine days after Samuel P. Langley's Aerodrome A *crashed into the Potomac (below), the Wright brothers achieved the world's first powered, man-carrying heavier-than-air flight at Kitty Hawk. At right, their plane, with Orville at the controls, rises into the air; Wilbur is running alongside. Both planes may be seen at the Smithsonian.*

Langley proudly in 1891, "is possible with engines we now possess."

Langley proceeded to the second stage of his investigation by building small flying machines to see if aerial lift could sustain them in actual powered flight. Though referred to as models, properly speaking they were not, for they were not modeled after anything in existence. Wings, propulsion, stabilizing devices, each part was a problem in engineering that Langley had to solve for himself. There was nothing to do but try and fail, and try again as one "aerodrome" (Langley's name for his aircraft) after another failed to fly. For five years the aging Secretary persevered through an almost continuous succession of failures that might have broken the will of younger men. When he set out with Alexander Graham Bell on May 6, 1896, to launch yet another aircraft from the roof of his Potomac houseboat, Langley scarcely dared to raise his hopes. Perhaps *Aerodrome Five*—thirteen feet in span and powered by a one-horsepower steam engine—would at least turn out to be an instructive failure. To his joy it was an inspiring success. It took off above the river and buzzed along for more than half a mile. When the fuel ran out after a minute and a half of flight, the aerodrome floated gently down to the water. Lifted out,

dried off, and refueled, it was again launched successfully. He had demonstrated, Langley said, not only the possibility, but also "the practicability of mechanical flight." It had been accomplished with only a small aircraft without a passenger, but the flight of *Aerodrome Five* that spring day sounded a clarion call. Human flight, in a stroke, had been rescued from almost universal disrepute. Langley had changed the whole climate of scholarly opinion. It was no coincidence that in 1899 the Smithsonian received a request for information about aeronautics from a young bicycle maker from Dayton, Ohio, named Wilbur Wright.

With this achievement, followed by an even better flight, of *Aerodrome Six*, in November of 1896, Langley rested content, having proved all that he had originally set out to prove. But fate, in the form of the Spanish-American War, intervened in 1898. The War Department, prodded by Assistant Secretary of the Navy Theodore Roosevelt, offered Langley a fifty-thousand-dollar grant to construct a man-carrying air machine. Another five years of exasperating experimenting ensued before Langley felt ready to make a first, modest trial flight. He had hoped to keep it as secret as possible, but there was little chance of that. All through the summer of 1903

Colonel Charles Lindbergh, above, stands beneath a wing of his famous Spirit of St. Louis, *now exhibited in the Smithsonian. Though a perennial favorite with visitors, the plane is also kept as a record of history; and some years ago the museum was closed for a day to enable Colonel Lindbergh, in the midst of writing a book, to climb back into the cockpit to check some fuel statistics that he had hastily jotted down on the instrument panel during his historic transatlantic flight.*

newspapermen had been lurking by the houseboat site thirty miles from Washington (where Langley was to conduct his test) and had been filing exuberant stories that were intended—apparently with malice aforethought, for the newsmen resented Langley's secretiveness—to raise expectations as high as possible. In 1903 most people were jeering Langley and his impudent challenge to the *status quo.* On October 7th, the aerodrome—"the Buzzard," journalists called it—was hoisted to the roof of the houseboat. Langley's brilliant engineer, Charles M. Manly, wearing a life preserver, got into the pilot's place and started up the powerful little engine he had helped to design and build. The signal to cut the catapult restraining cable was given and then observers heard a harsh, grinding noise, and the aircraft was snarled in the catapult. "It simply slid into the water like a handful of mortar," reported the Washington *Post* with glee. Jubilation was somewhat muted, however. It was clear that the Buzzard had not yet been fairly tested. On December 8th, nine days before the Wright brothers would achieve immortality on the sand dunes of Kitty Hawk, Langley's plane was launched once more. This time the back wings and tail were smashed in the launching and the machine swooped upward, looped over, and crashed

into the water. "Any stout boy of fifteen toughening winters," announced the *Post,* "could have skimmed an oyster shell much farther." The nation's press, followed in turn by vaudeville comedians and comic cartoonists, rained a chorus of mockery down upon the professor and his foolish flying machine. "The jeering became a kind of triumphant ecstasy," observed Mark Sullivan in *Our Times.* Ambrose Bierce, for example, wrote that flying would "require an atmosphere a little denser than the intelligence of one scientist and not quite so dense as that of two." What should have been merely a preliminary trial had become for Langley a final, hideous, public humiliation. Perhaps Sullivan summed it up best: Langley "had the tragic fate of deepening in a spectacular way the average man's conviction that human flight could never be." What was most galling of all to Langley was that he lost all chances to vindicate his work. The War Department, fearful of the public outcry, refused to support him any more. Heartbroken, the seventy-year-old scientist returned to astrophysics. In 1906 he died, but his ill-fated aircraft would appear once more as a *cause célèbre.*

Langley's loyal friends at the Smithsonian, including Dr. Charles Walcott, the fourth Secretary, never stopped asking themselves the

CONTINUED ON PAGE 65

Samuel Pierpont Langley: Toward a New Astronomy

In 1864, a few years after two German physicists, Kirchhoff and Bunsen, had laid the groundwork for a "new astronomy" by devising the spectroscopic method of analyzing light, a promising young Chicago architect named Samuel Pierpont Langley gave up his business and went to Europe for a year of study, determined to become a full-time astronomer. Rapidly he rose to the top of his profession, and when, in 1887, at the age of fifty-two, he was invited by Secretary Baird to join the Smithsonian and build an Astrophysical Observatory in Washington, he had already crossed the farthest boundaries of scientific knowledge.

Baird's policy in hiring Langley was to restore the delicate balance at the Institution between the physical and biological sciences, so recently upset by the young "Bairdians" of the natural history division. Yet if Langley was brought to the Smithsonian to revive the glories of an earlier day—when the physicist Joseph Henry was Secretary—he was also, more importantly, the forerunner of a new scientific era. Conservative in dress and stiffly formal in manner (even, it seems, while observing a solar eclipse, opposite), he was nonetheless endowed with a prophetic cast of mind. His scientific prose alone spoke eloquently of his character. Contemptuous of the Victorians' taste for ornament, he cultivated a lean, modern rhythm. "Today we hunt for tigers," he would intone by way of illustration. "Tomorrow we shall hunt for bears."

There was nothing novel in the idea of a Smithsonian observatory. It had first been proposed more than fifty years before by John Quincy Adams, a distant relative of Langley. But times had changed, and Adams's classical science of celestial mapping no longer satisfied forward-looking astronomers of Langley's day. "The prime object of astronomy until lately," Secretary Langley observed, "has been to say *where* any heavenly body is, rather than *what* it is . . . ." Indifferent to mere positional astronomy, the new astrophysicists wanted to understand the very structure and properties of celestial objects. The sun was Langley's most absorbing interest, but he did not care to mark its precise place in the sky. Instead, he sought first to find out what it was made of, next to map the distribution of its heat, and finally to explain "how it affects the earth and the wants of man," the weather and the harvests.

Altogether it was a very different kind of scientific enterprise. Even the traditional telescope was put aside, displaced by smaller instruments to measure light. And, more significantly, the new astronomy did not profess to know all the answers. Gone was the old Newtonian cosmos, governed by simple laws that scientists could hope to comprehend; in its place was a vast, mysterious universe, only fragments of which were accessible to the tiny minds of men. Feeling the rush of a new age upon him, Langley became a skeptic, wary of affirming anything but bits and pieces of his studies, offering only tentative estimates of how much heat the sun gives off, and how much reaches the earth. "We must not consider," he reflected, "that anything is absolutely settled or true. . . ." The very laws of nature could not be trusted, "for the things that we see from day to day appear permanent only by comparison with the duration of our own brief life, and our own little experience."

He was sixty-five when the century ended, but he saw clearly what lay ahead, with a youthful enthusiasm that belied his years. Even to his death, in 1906, just one year after Einstein announced his theory of relativity, Langley pronounced himself untroubled by the new, unsettling universe that his research had begun to illuminate. To the end he remained a daring pioneer. And, with unruffled aplomb, he firmly led the Smithsonian into the twentieth century.

The first flight of Robert Goddard's liquid-fuel rocket (above) took place in March, 1926, on his Aunt Effie's farm in Massachusetts. Describing the launch, Goddard said "It looked almost magical as it rose, without any appreciably greater noise or flame, as if it said: 'I've been here long enough; I think I'll be going somewhere else, if you don't mind.'"

Dr. Goddard constructed the tower above in the 1930's in New Mexico. This photograph was taken by his wife.

COURTESY OF ESTHER C. GODDARD

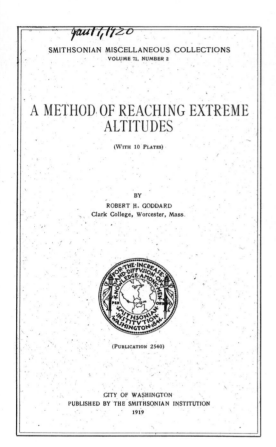

SMITHSONIAN MISCELLANEOUS COLLECTIONS
VOLUME 71, NUMBER 2

A METHOD OF REACHING EXTREME ALTITUDES

(WITH 10 PLATES)

BY
ROBERT H. GODDARD
Clark College, Worcester, Mass.

(PUBLICATION 2540)

CITY OF WASHINGTON
PUBLISHED BY THE SMITHSONIAN INSTITUTION
1919

Goddard's theories on rocketry arrived at the Smithsonian in a wooden box. Dr. Charles Abbot, who was then studying solar radiation, called the paper "the best presentation of a research project" he had seen, and it was published (left) in 1919 as part of the Institution's program for the "diffusion of knowledge." In the picture above, Professor Goddard stands before a blackboard in a classroom at Clark University, explaining to students his thesis on how man would one day reach the moon.

CONTINUED FROM PAGE 61

unsettled question: Could Samuel Langley's plane really fly? In 1914 the pioneer aviator Glenn Curtiss was persuaded to attempt one final test flight of the plane. After making some modifications—crucial ones, as Orville Wright pointed out bitterly—Curtiss got the Buzzard to fly a few hundred feet. Langley's friends were delighted—perhaps too delighted, for in 1918 the aircraft was displayed at the Smithsonian with a label identifying it as "the first man-carrying aeroplane in the history of the world capable of sustained free flight." With that, a bitter feud that had smoldered for years broke out in earnest between Orville Wright (his brother died in 1912) and the Smithsonian Institution. It reached its climax in 1928 when Wright sent his historic Kitty Hawk *Flyer* to the South Kensington Museum in London. That year Dr. Charles G. Abbot became the fifth Secretary of the Smithsonian Institution and began his patient, diplomatic efforts to patch up the unseemly feud. The offensive label was taken off, and on two occasions public apologies were made. In 1942 seventy-one-year-old Orville Wright relented; the Smithsonian, he felt, had repaired the injustice. In 1948 the *Wright Flyer* was brought home to America and to the Smithsonian.

Throughout those years of dispute, Langley's memory was being preserved at the Smithsonian in more fruitful ways. Back in 1895, when Abbot arrived at the Astrophysical Observatory, he had been captivated by Langley's belief that the sun's radiation was the key to understanding the weather. By 1904 Langley and Abbot had good reason to believe that the sun, so steady and serene to the casual observer, was not quite so steady as men thought. There seemed to be some variation in the amount of heat it sent out to the earth. Skeptics at first doubted that such solar variation existed. It was so slight, they contended, that it could be written off as an observational error due to atmospheric conditions. There was nothing for Abbot to do but push on with the work in an area where atmospheric interference was at a minimum. It would have been best, of course, to have gotten an observation post entirely beyond the earth's atmosphere. Failing that, Abbot and his assistants began an odd hunt throughout the world in search of blue skies. They took the sun's measurement in such places as the Atacama Desert, in Chile, and near an all-but-abandoned monastery in the Sinai desert, so isolated it had served as a Christian sanctuary since the days of the Roman persecutions.

The work had not gone on long when, in 1916, the Smithsonian

received a letter which any other scientific organization might easily have filed and forgotten. To Abbot, however, it seemed a godsend. The author described his attempts to build a rocket that could reach very high altitudes. He was, however, desperate for funds: "I feel that it is to the Smithsonian Institution alone that I must look, now that I cannot continue the work unassisted." The writer was Robert H. Goddard, a reputable physicist from Worcester, Massachusetts, with a project so "disreputable" he dared not disclose its full scope. Since the time he was seventeen, and an avid reader of H. G. Wells, Goddard had been working with fanatic fixity of purpose to build a rocket that could reach into outer space. In a long report submitted to the Smithsonian, he detailed the years and years of mathematical and engineering calculations that proved, at least to himself, that a rocket could be sent a hundred miles into space. Prompted by Abbot, the Smithsonian granted Goddard five thousand dollars to pursue his work. It was a remarkable act of faith, for the research had no precedent anywhere. For four-teen years, with a total of about $15,000, the Smithsonian supported Goddard in his lone-wolf researches, and Goddard would confide the results of his work to no one else. He learned in 1919 what

could happen when the public heard of his rockets. That year the Smithsonian published his epoch-making essay on *A Method of Reaching Extreme Altitudes*. When word got out that a crackpot scientist, backed by the Smithsonian, was attempting to reach the moon, the press descended upon Worcester in search of the "moon-rocket man." Goddard was suddenly a figure on the front page of every American newspaper, and people began offering themselves to him as passengers for the first space flight. Then Tin Pan Alley pitched in with a new novelty tune about "moon rockets," and Mary Pickford's press agent wired Goddard that "America's Sweetheart" would like to send the first message to the moon.

To Goddard what was most trying about the publicity was that he had not yet launched a rocket higher than a man could throw a baseball. It was many years before he would. In 1925, in fact, working at his Aunt Effie's farm in Massachusetts, he became so discouraged with his lack of progress that he wondered if he should accept a five-hundred-dollar check from the Smithsonian. Then, on March 16, 1926, Goddard made history. A ten-foot-long rocket powered by liquid oxygen and gasoline rose off the launching stand—about forty feet up. Not precisely "extreme altitudes," he

The close-up of a lunar eclipse, at left, was taken by one of the Smithsonian Astrophysical Observatory's Baker-Nunn cameras. As Goddard's dream of landing on the moon becomes a realistic goal, lunar studies have been stepped up—with the observatory taking a large part in the research. Meteoritics, another field in which the observatory pioneers, is pursued with highly sophisticated equipment. At right a scientist examines the external structure of a meteorite. Behind him is a mass spectrometer used for examination of isotopic composition and intricate measurements of noble gases in meteorites. The chunk of metal at lower right came from Sputnik IV. In analyzing the piece of the satellite, observatory scientists found it had picked up traces of wustite and akaganeite, two minerals rarely found on the earth.

admitted to Abbot, yet this was a landmark as important as Kitty Hawk; it was the first liquid-fuel rocket ever to fly.

Before German experimenters were under way with their work, Goddard had patented many fundamental features of the modern rocket. Indeed, some Germans, via two Goddard articles published by the Smithsonian and copies of patents, had become aware of his work. "Dr. Goddard was ahead of us all," said Wernher von Braun many years later. By the time World War II broke out, Goddard's rockets were racing nine thousand feet into the air at speeds of seven hundred miles per hour, but unlike Germany the American Government never supported rocket research; it seemed too remote from any practical military use. The space age had already begun, but Goddard was not to be a part of it. In August, 1945, at the age of sixty-three, he died. His greatest honors were all posthumous.

As far as Abbot's solar research was concerned, his years of valiant support for Goddard had no practical reward. Abbot continued his own work, to be sure, even to the extent of founding an entirely new Smithsonian division devoted to studying the way in which radiation affects life on earth (see p. 70). Working on his own, he discovered that the variation in the sun's radiation follows

a regular pattern of fluctuation. But while Dr. Abbot continued his solar research, the new age of rocketry he had helped to nurture was moving the Astrophysical Observatory into entirely new endeavors. Recently, the observatory broke sharply with its past—in a revolution brought about by rockets, satellites, high-speed computers, and a Harvard professor of astronomy, Fred L. Whipple.

Chosen as director of the observatory in 1955, Dr. Whipple promptly announced a new direction for the Smithsonian bureau: It was to "embrace not only research in solar activity and its effects upon the earth, but also meteoritic studies and studies of the high atmosphere." The headquarters of the bureau were moved to the grounds of the Harvard College Observatory, and Whipple set about organizing a task which, at first glance, hardly seemed related to meteoritics: keeping track of the artificial satellites planned for launching during the International Geophysical Year.

The tracking technique Whipple developed included a new telescopic camera called the Baker-Nunn—a device capable of photographing a satellite six inches in diameter whirling more than twenty-five hundred miles above the earth (the equivalent of photographing a speeding .30-caliber bullet two hundred miles away).

The Astrophysical Observatory operates a dozen Baker-Nunn camera installations around the world like the one at left in Jupiter, Florida. Its triaxial mounting permits the camera to move quickly, and with sharp precision, to follow the paths of fast-moving comets and satellites. The photograph above, taken by an installation in Australia, shows the satellite Pegasus streaking through stars of the Canis Major constellation.

The technique included, too, a network of amateur observers, reminiscent of the task force Joseph Henry had created for his weather observations. Known as Moonwatch, Whipple's forces were deployed throughout the world to supplement, with their sightings, the precise optical observations made by the dozen Baker-Nunn stations. To keep up with the orbits of the fast-moving satellites, Whipple then recruited an IBM-704 computer. (One of the observatory's scientists, to illustrate the value of these high-speed computers in modern astronomy, used another IBM to calculate an orbit for the planet Mars. Working with the same data used by the seventeenth-century astronomer Kepler, the computer took eight seconds to solve the problem; it had taken Kepler two years.) When Sputnik I was launched in 1957, Moonwatch was the first observation network to pick it up.

Today the observatory does not merely keep track of satellites; it has moved on to Whipple's more sophisticated goals through studies of the complex forces that play on the man-made objects. Perturbations in the orbits, for example, have yielded new discoveries. Some irregularities are caused by variations in the gravitational field of the earth. Spotting those subtle shifts, researchers

have come upon new notions of what lies at the interior of the earth. Other irregularities result from the resistance of the atmosphere and so give measurements of the relative density of the atmosphere hundreds of miles higher than any observation balloons have gone. Simultaneous observations of a satellite by two tracking stations permit simple geometrical triangulation, producing the most precise measurement yet of distances on the earth—a measurement designated the Smithsonian Standard Earth.

Most recently the observatory has set up a sixteen-camera network covering two and a half billion acres in the Midwest. Called Prairie Network, it is expected to photograph meteors as they fall toward earth. With such photographs researchers should be able to determine the origin of the meteorites. Biochemists will study the freshly-fallen objects for traces of extraterrestrial life. Whipple will study them for evidence of the origins of the solar system.

The observatory, under Whipple's direction, has become one of the Smithsonian's largest bureaus, with a combined Harvard-Smithsonian staff that includes perhaps as many as 10 per cent of all the country's Ph.D.'s in astronomy. It has become, too, a center for some of the most arresting research in all modern science. Dr.

Members of a "Moonwatch" team, at left, watch for orbiting satellites. Originally set up to spot man-made objects as they were first launched, Moonwatch now keeps a lookout for disintegrating satellites as well, to assist in recovering the precious fragments that fall back from space.

Whipple, for example, proposes launching a block of dry ice into space to create an artificial comet. The idea seems ordinary enough, but, knowing his own comet's composition, and studying the tail it makes, Whipple will be able to make comparisons with natural comets for clues to the very elements that make up the universe. As for the natural comets, he suggests probing one with a space vehicle to make tests. The observatory already launches packages of pellets (in what is called Project Celescope) which are blasted back toward earth, with the flaming descent of these man-made meteors observed through Super-Schmidt cameras. In a joint project with Britain's Jodrell Bank radio telescope, the observatory is studying flare stars. Then, too, the observatory is working on orbiting astronomical observatories, satellites in space that can make observations undistorted by the atmosphere that blankets the earth. Nor is the observatory neglecting exobiology, the study of life in outer space. As one of the Smithsonian's bold young scientists has said, "Preliminary results seem to suggest that the origin of life is a general process, occurring on all planets [possibly as many as a million in the Milky Way alone] with extensive reducing atmospheres in an appropriate temperature range. . . . Within these limits, and

in this view, life must be a pervasive component of the universe."

The pieces of knowledge gathered by the Astrophysical Observatory, and the truths they lead to, seem decidedly esoteric. At the very least they are a long way from the comfortable familiarity of Joseph Henry's weather maps. Henry could not have foreseen that his Institution would one day be analyzing the tiniest bits of cosmic dust, and the smallest specks of meteorites, to discover truths about the universe. Yet he had made certain that such work would be a part of the Smithsonian. In 1870, when Henry refused to print William Poole's *Index to Periodical Literature*, Poole lashed out at the Secretary and his unaccountable preoccupation with research, and particularly with "'the preparation of a new orbit for the planet Neptune!' The old one is probably worn out. Let the planet be supplied without delay with so proper an appendage . . . it may be butting against our planet and disturbing generally . . . the solar system . . . the world ought to know what the most useless institution in creation is doing and proposing to do." The Institution, quite simply, proposed to set no limits on what might be considered useful research. It proposed instead to support dreamers like Langley, Goddard, and Whipple.

Sunlight
And the Secrets of Life

The Smithsonian's fifth Secretary, Charles Abbot, at his desk in a tower room of the old Smithsonian Building, founded the radiation laboratory in 1929.

"It is now well understood," wrote Samuel Pierpont Langley in 1897, "that. . .every manifestation of life from that of the lowest vegetable form up through animal existence, to that of man, including all his works and industries, comes from the sun. . . ." So broad a principle was easy to announce, but the task that Secretary Langley bequeathed to his successors was far more arduous—to spell out in precise terms the "unexpected relations" that the sun bears to the earth. Now, almost seventy years later, researchers at the Smithsonian are still trying to explain the ways that solar energy affects living creatures on earth, experimenting with such elementary forms of life as the tiny single-celled organisms in the culture vessel opposite, which these scientists use to study only one of many subtle plant responses—the phototropic process by which plants bend toward a source of light.

Radiation research was first given official status at the Smithsonian in 1929 when Secretary Abbot founded a Division of Radiation and Organisms within the Astrophysical Observatory. And in 1965 this division, housed in the basement of the old Smithsonian Building (and also in a sunny greenhouse out back), was finally made an independent unit of the Institution and was renamed the Radiation Biology Laboratory.

The radiation experts at the Smithsonian are interested, above all, in plant life, and hope to learn exactly how and why it responds to the different quantities and qualities of solar energy that reach the surface of the earth. They know that sunlight, by the low-energy process called photoregulation, can alter the structure and behavior of plants. And, by the process known as photosynthesis, sunbeams also provide the radiant energy that green plants convert to carbohydrates, the basic food of all living creatures on earth.

While the radiation laboratory investigates other phenomena (the lethal power of ultraviolet light, for example), it is the photoregulatory and photosynthetic processes that most obviously shape man's environment. And so, with an eye toward one day controlling the intricate forces of nature, the Smithsonian's radiation biologists would like to understand just what amounts of sunlight make different plants respond in different ways; which of the variously colored portions of the spectrum are most efficient in promoting these effects; and what mechanisms within the plants themselves actually make them react as they do.

Progress in this field must necessarily come piecemeal from laborious studies of individual specimens. Radiation experimenters

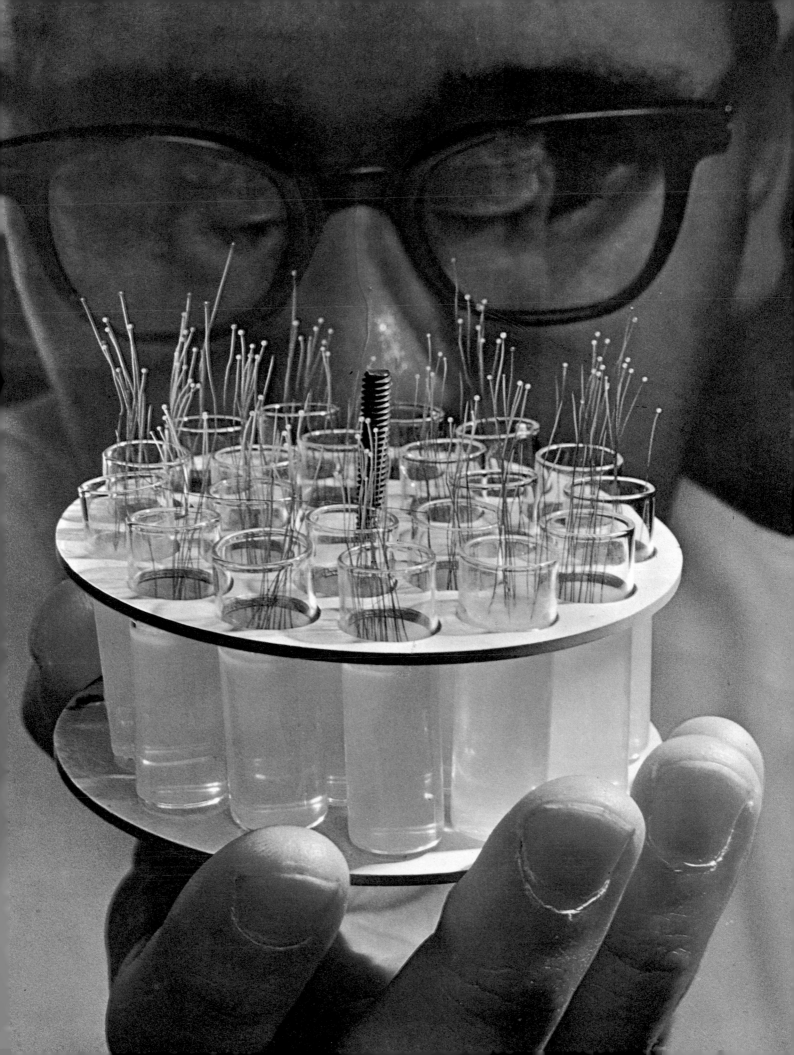

A greenhouse at the Radiation Biology Laboratory is used to analyze plant growth. Plants are grown in sunlight (below) with all changes in humidity, intensity of light, and other variables scrupulously recorded (above). In sealed rooms like the one at left, nature is duplicated exactly—except for a lighting system that excludes part of the solar spectrum.

have run tests, for example, in a series of artificial "growth chambers," each of which was made to duplicate the entire spectrum of natural light by means of a row of fifteen 15-watt fluorescent tubes, topped by four incandescent lamps. What these researchers have discovered is that when beans are grown in a room where the incandescent lighting has been turned off, the plants grow 25 to 30 per cent less in height. This result they explain by noting that the incandescent lamps alone provide far-red light, located near the long wave end of the visible spectrum. And it is this kind of light, they conclude, that controls the elongation of the beans.

The radiation laboratory has also tried to measure the photoregulatory effect on plants of different quantities of light. By artificially lengthening the day, for instance, experimenters have postponed the flowering of "short day" plants like the poinsettia, and have so manipulated the most rudimentary habits of nature. "In the foreseeable future," says Dr. William Klein, director of the laboratory, "enough knowledge may be gathered to understand and control the effects of radiation on biological systems."

Toward this goal, in the long run, it is the mysterious photosynthetic effect that may yield the most dramatic results to radiation scientists. So far, photosynthesis, the process by which light stimulates plants to take up carbon dioxide from the air and transform it into sugar, is the sole known means of producing food on earth, and at best this process is only 3 or 4 per cent efficient. The laboratory has already shown that various portions of the spectrum can be more effective than others in promoting photosynthesis—that red light, for example, makes wheat plants assimilate the greatest quantities of carbon dioxide. And presently the laboratory is studying the development of a component of green plants called the chloroplast, which carries the pigment (chlorophyll) that absorbs radiant energy in photosynthesis. Eventually the radiation experts hope to explain completely the complicated mechanism by which plants actually photosynthesize.

No one can predict with certainty where this research will lead, but its potentialities are staggering. If, in the future, scientists learn enough to duplicate artificially the photosynthetic process, the impact upon the economy of this planet will be immense. Atomic power, a former president of M.I.T. once noted, "has greater interest for the public imagination. . . . But who can say whether the answer to the secret of photosynthesis may not have more far-reaching effects on our lives and those of generations to come?"

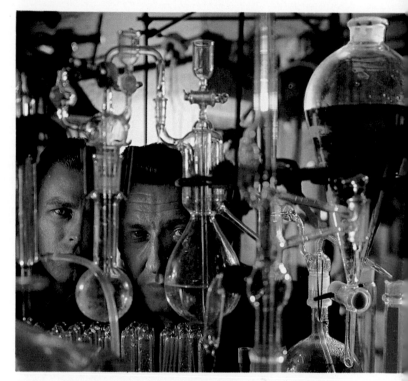

In the marine biology laboratory, William Klein (at right, above), the director of the Radiation Biology Laboratory, checks an experiment on marine plant life. The researcher below examines a specimen to be submitted to a carbon-14 dating device. The dating laboratory, administered by Klein, dates specimens for all bureaus of the Smithsonian.

BOTH PHOTOGRAPHS BY ARNOLD NEWMAN

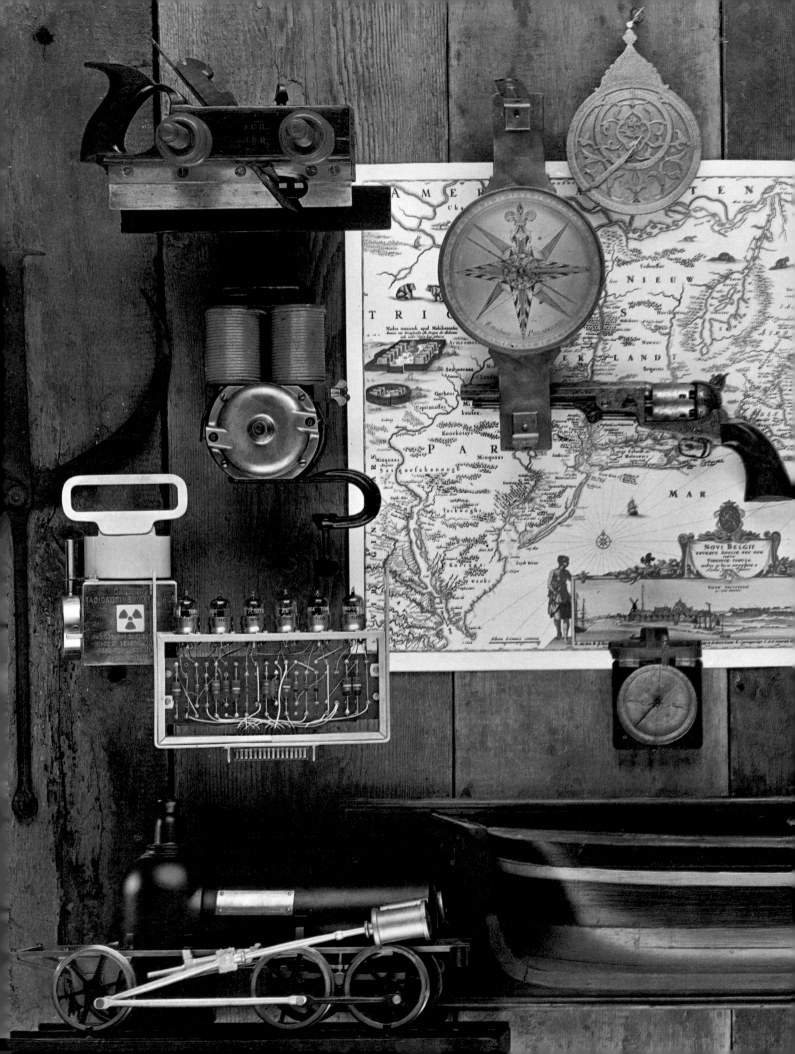

Moments of America's history are highlighted at left with items like the Colt revolver at center, George Washington's compass (above the revolver), an antique astrolabe, a map of seventeenth-century New England, a compass used by Lewis and Clark (below the map). The map is surrounded by a Queen Anne doll, a carpenter's plane, a computer part, a patent model of the Baldwin locomotive, a silver coffeepot, and a model of the Baltimore Clipper.

PHOTOGRAPH BY ARNOLD NEWMAN

Chapter Four

A HISTORY WRITTEN IN OBJECTS

75

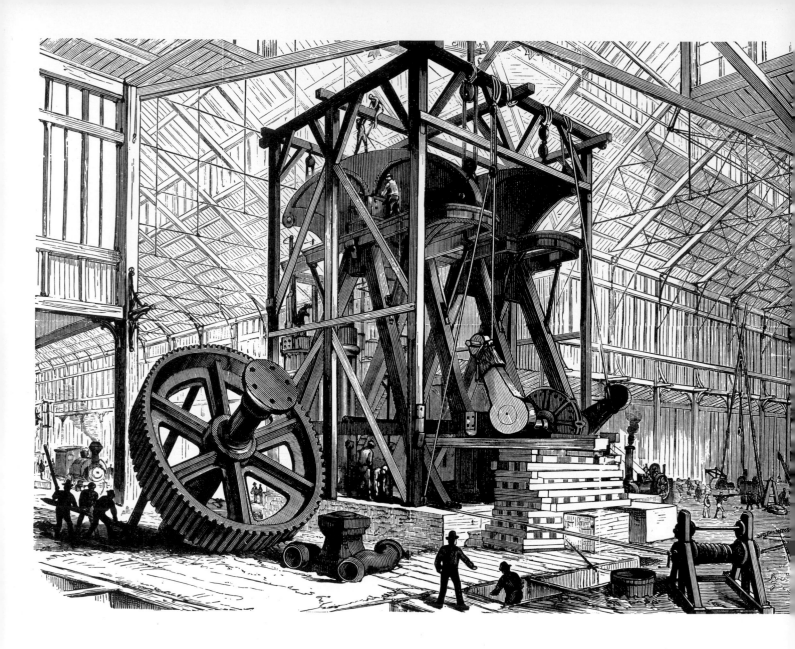

The Smithsonian's Museum of History and Technology is, essentially, a history book written in objects. A choice selection of period rooms documents the history of domestic life in America. Campaign buttons, posters, and banners give substance to a part of America's political history. Stamps are transformed into postal history, coins into monetary history, cars and coaches and locomotives into a history of transportation. The progress of technology is recorded in hundreds of patent models, and in particularly precious items like Whitney's cotton gin, Edison's light bulb, and Morse's telegraph.

Officially opened in 1964, the new History and Technology Building is the product of the Smithsonian's century of experience and experimentation in making museums for the enlightenment of scholars and the pleasure of visitors. It bears the stamp of several Secretaries—among them Samuel Langley. In the original Smithsonian Building, Langley had once opened a special room for children. Speaking on behalf of the children, "and as one of them," Langley said at the inauguration ceremonies, "I should say that we never have a fair chance in museums . . . most of the things we . . . would like to know about have Latin words on them which we cannot understand. . . . Some great philosopher has said that 'knowledge begins in wonder'. . . . If I may speak of myself, I am sure I remember how the whole studies of my life have been colored by one or two strong impressions received in childhood." The new museum bears, too, the unmistakable mark of one of Spencer Baird's young assistants, George Brown Goode. One of the few people in the nineteenth century to make a penetrating study of museums (see p. 80), Goode declared emphatically that the museum of the future must be "a nursery of living thought," not "a cemetery of bric-a-brac."

It was, precisely, with a cemetery of bric-a-brac that the Smithsonian's Museum of History and Technology began in 1876, the year of the Philadelphia Centennial Exposition. A stupendously large world's fair commemorating the one hundredth birthday of America, the exposition was intended to represent, according to one observer, "the flower and first fruition of the seed planted by patriotism." As visitors were given to understand in 1876, the flower was made of iron, and the first fruit was the machine.

On the 240-acre fairgrounds along the Schuylkill River, exhibits numbered in the thousands. Even the Smithsonian had sent a dis-

The tattered Star-Spangled Banner is restored, at left, in 1914. Too large (twenty by thirty-eight feet) to be displayed in its full proportions in the crowded Arts and Industries Building, the flag now hangs, fully unfurled, in the Smithsonian's new Museum of History and Technology.

A curator of political history, Wilcomb Washburn, at right, examines materials documenting the election of 1900. Only a few such objects are put on public display; many more are kept in special archives for historians.

write what is now the national anthem, and which was loaned in 1909 by a descendant of Fort McHenry's commanding officer, was turned over permanently to the Smithsonian. In 1912 Mrs. William Howard Taft donated a dress to the costume collection and, by 1914, the museum was able to open an exhibit containing fifteen dresses formerly belonging to First Ladies. Soon the deluge of gift giving filled all the available space, and, by 1924, the Smithsonian Regents made the first of many appeals to Congress for a full-fledged "Museum of Engineering and Industry." A handful of curators continued to labor, without adequate quarters, through the Federal Government's concern with economy in the twenties, the Great Depression of the thirties, and the austerity of the war years.

In 1953, Leonard Carmichael was appointed the seventh Secretary of the Smithsonian. A former college professor and professional psychologist, he was, too, a keen administrator. He immediately presented Congress with the discovery that Federal appropriations, apart from those designated for salaries, had decreased since 1933 —when the dollar was worth considerably more. Spurred by Carmichael, the Smithsonian won from Congress a generous chance for revitalization. In 1955, the first installment of what would even-

tually be a $36,000,000 appropriation was given to the Institution for the construction of a new Museum of History and Technology. The long wait had had some advantages; scholarship in Goode's discipline had been growing, and a considerably enlarged museum staff, led by Frank A. Taylor, was well prepared to build the sort of comprehensive museum Goode had envisioned. And Secretary Carmichael added a capping goal: The new museum was planned "to deepen the content of American patriotism."

In creating a museum that is, root and branch, historical, the Smithsonian's curators face subtle problems. The heart of the museum's collections is gifts from private donors; the Institution seldom purchases museum articles unless a benefactor donates funds for that specific purpose. To create valuable collections, then, is a diplomatic challenge. Gifts of curiosities must be turned aside artfully; and objects of special worth which may be on their way to a pawnshop or to another museum must be won with equal persuasiveness by the curators. The museum has been offered such treasures as an old pair of shoes (with an explanatory note, "My friends tell me these are something a museum should have."), a variety of "rare coins" that turn out to be toy money, and Confederate bills

CONTINUED ON PAGE 82

George Brown Goode:
Building a "House Full of Ideas"

George Brown Goode's father, a retired merchant, kept a set of Smithsonian *Reports* in his library, and it was from reading these weighty volumes as a boy that the younger Goode first learned of the Smithsonian, and dreamed of working there one day. Before many years had passed, he secured a job as an assistant curator arranging specimens for Spencer Fullerton Baird; and by 1887, at the age of thirty-five, he had attained the rank of Assistant Secretary, charged with supervising the National Museum.

"Museum administration," Goode was later to observe, "has become one of the learned professions. . . ." Indeed, if any single man had made it so, it was this energetic young ichthyologist, turned museum expert, pictured at right. Under his guiding hand, the Smithsonian enlarged its collections to fifteen times what they had been before, and increased a museum staff of thirteen to a force of more than two hundred. Not only was Goode master of the National Museum, but he represented both the Smithsonian and the Federal Government at a wide variety of international expositions, from the Philadelphia Centennial of 1876 to the Columbian Historical Exposition of 1892–1893 in Madrid. A brilliant organizer, he planned his pavilions with such care that he could set them up in a matter of hours, much to the astonishment of other exhibitors. And always he designed the content of his displays to please the audiences that would see them—as when he offered Madrid an exhibit illustrating the conditions of human and animal life in America at the time the Spanish discovered the New World.

From these far-flung expositions, too, he brought back objects to enrich his own museum—musical instruments, ecclesiastical art, incunabula, medals, ivories, autographs, and assorted Americana. Yet he never collected at random. "An efficient educational museum," he often said, "may be described as a collection of instructive labels, each illustrated by a well-selected specimen." And it was education that Goode saw as his most urgent mission. While recognizing that a museum could be a powerful tool of scholarly research, he was also alert to the new democratic age, and sought to tap "the possibilities for public enlightenment" implicit in his museum. Armed with detailed plans for "a people's museum" that would teach by means of "object lessons," Goode envisioned a systematic "house full of ideas" that would instruct as well as entertain the crowds that visited the Smithsonian.

"Considerations of upholstery," as a friend derisively called them, were never too mundane to engage Goode's attention. Clearly printed labels, restful interior colors, simple cabinets, efficient lighting, all were prescribed in minute detail to advance his program of education. There was even a provision for comfortable seats included in his grand design, "for the task of the museum visitor is a weary one at best."

Goode died at the age of forty-five, before he could make the National Museum conform completely to his principles. But his ideas were taken up by museum men around the world. "Many so-called museums," he once remarked, "are little more than storehouses filled with the materials of which museums are made." More than half a century later, the seventh Secretary of the Smithsonian Institution, Leonard Carmichael, set out to finish what Goode's untimely death had left undone. "Our old display method," Carmichael said, "simply amounted to visual storage." And, reviving principles that Goode had been the first to formulate, Secretary Carmichael, a psychologist by training, envisioned the new Museum of History and Technology as an instrument of public education, to transform the vast Smithsonian collections into "a living textbook" on the Mall.

PHOTOGRAPH BY ARNOLD NEWMAN

CONTINUED FROM PAGE 79

printed by cereal manufacturers as giveaways. Once, after a tempting magazine article had appeared informing readers that they might have gold in their own back yards, the Smithsonian was inundated with tons of gravel.

The museum curators are not at all given to joking about such matters. Unsolicited gifts have too frequently turned out to be rare artifacts that fill a gap in a collection; and private donations form the basis of most of the museum's finest collections, which, in turn, form the archives from which objects are taken for displays. Recently, private collectors have turned over a comprehensive collection of rare Jacquard-woven silk pictures, several dozen pieces of Early American glassware, cameras (including one purchased in the 1930's by William Randolph Hearst that was specially designed to photograph the electrocution of Ruth Snyder from a concealed position), an improvised nuclear reactor made of two tons of fuel in a pickle barrel used for research at New York University. There seems to be a collector somewhere in the world for every conceivable sort of object; and the collectors appear to be delighted to see the Museum of History and Technology transmute their hobbies into history. The War Department and other branches of the Federal Government have always been notably generous to the museum. The Patent Office, for example (see p. 90), has over the years given the Smithsonian the best of its priceless collection of patent models—contrivances that inventors were once required to submit to the Government along with their patent claims.

Yet, for all this generosity, curators do not simply sit back and wait for windfalls. Recently, for example, the curator of the Department of Cultural History decided to repair what he felt was a serious omission in the physical record of America's domestic history. He set out for California's Mother Lode country at the foothills of the Sierra Nevada to find a settler's kitchen surviving from the days of the Gold Rush. He canvassed country museums, antique shops, local historical societies, and even the Park Service; but he found nothing. However, knowing from long experience and practiced intuition what might have furnished such a house, he was able to pick up an occasional piece of kitchenware. There was little to go on; California life in 1850 is known only little better than the life of New England in 1750. Finally, two years after his first expedition, a California woman heard of his search and led him to her great-grandfather's home. It had been abandoned for half a

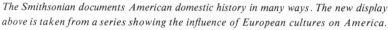

The Smithsonian documents American domestic history in many ways. The new display above is taken from a series showing the influence of European cultures on America.

The room opposite, one of the popular displays of "Gowns of the First Ladies," is furnished with rosewood chairs made by the nineteenth-century manufacturer J. H. Belter. Mary Todd Lincoln's tea service is at center. The mannequins represent, from left to right, Mary Todd Lincoln, Jane Appleton Pierce, Abigail Fillmore, Betty Taylor Bliss (Zachary Taylor's daughter), Sarah Polk, and Harriet Lane (President Buchanan's niece).

Curators in the field of domestic history collect entire rooms as well as individual objects. The eighteenth-century apothecary shop at left, with its ornate ceiling and rococo jars, was brought piece by piece from Freiburg, Germany. An adobe dwelling of the same period, above, was reconstructed from houses found in the area of Santa Fe. Its furnishings combine Spanish and Indian styles.

century, and it was empty save for a plucky coat of blue paint. But the shaded areas of the paint showed where the kitchen furnishings had been placed. Piece by piece the room was dismantled, shipped back to the Smithsonian, and reassembled there in the spring of 1965—furnished with the vintage pickings from the curator's tour of northern California junk shops.

But the curator's work does not stop with mere acquisition. To discover just how one Early American bedroom should be outfitted, a curator searched through three-hundred-year-old court records to find what the original owner had bequeathed in his will to his heirs. To determine the sort of lettering to be used on a sign for a restored mid-nineteenth-century instrument-maker's shop, curators found that the only authentic guide was the sign over McSorley's saloon in New York City. To provide an eighteenth-century sugar loaf for one period room, curators sought out a bakery in Antwerp that was making sugar loaves today exactly as it had been making them for two hundred years. The careful search through old records, the tour of the West Coast, and the educated imagination that leads a historian to Antwerp are typical of the sort of work that yields such collections as the museum's "Hall of Everyday Life in Early

America." America's domestic history is portrayed through displays of kitchen utensils or pottery or glassware intended to show, in a systematic way, the manner in which American life was first shaped (and continues to be influenced) by the early colonists from Europe. And a representative number of period rooms, preserved with such touches as an open book next to a comfortable chair, irresistibly bring to life the story of America's first hardy settlers. The rooms encompass a broad sample of American life—from a seventeenth-century Massachusetts schoolroom (with signs admonishing LOVE ONE ANOTHER and SWEAR NOT AT ALL) to a nineteenth-century ice-cream parlor from Georgetown in Washington.

The record of progress in technology is frequently more difficult to come by than the museum's articles of domestic and political history. Although old furnishings and utensils are in constant danger of being discarded, there is a good chance that families will keep them out of sentimental, if not historical, interest. Politics and war are usually accompanied by fanfare, and even the least likely mementos are saved by people with a sense of their historical value. But revolutions in the history of manufacturing often pass unnoticed. Pioneer achievements may be represented by the most trivial

America's military history is recorded at the Smithsonian with memorabilia like the flags above from the Mexican War. The national flag of Mexico (left) was captured in battle; the flag to the right was carried by Company I, 4th Regiment, Indiana Volunteers. The rapid-fire Gatling gun, in a small patent model at right, was invented in 1862; it is the forerunner of the modern machine gun.

PHOTOGRAPH BY ARNOLD NEWMAN

of enterprises. The sort of sophisticated manipulation of metal that now permits exceptionally complex industrial feats was originated by men manufacturing such gadgets as bottle caps.

One of the most notable exhibits in the Museum of History and Technology is that of a machine shop. Housed in a roughhewn room built in 1829 as part of a Connecticut clock factory, the shop contains planing machines, drills, lathes, and other tools typical of the last century. Casual visitors to the exhibit see the sort of place in which their grandfathers might have worked; those better versed in history will see an archetypal example of the workshop in which America began to create its mighty industrial system. The expert sees even more, for each of the shop's machines represents a landmark in the road to the manufacture of interchangeable machine parts—the essence of mass production, and the foundation of the greatest technological system ever devised.

It is no small feat to create such a room. Historic machines of the sort displayed are exceedingly rare; unlike "classic cars," classic lathes are usually junked. Most of the counterparts of the exhibited machines were, in fact, melted down for ordnance in the Civil and Mexican wars. Scouring the countryside for eight years, Smithso-

nian historians uncovered them in New England hamlets and abandoned factories; one was found buried underground. Any home mechanic knows a turret lathe when he sees one, but few people know what the first turret lathe looked like. It is an object surely as important in its way as Morse's telegraph; yet the antique machines have left behind no record, except perhaps in the rising prosperity of some Vermont factory that vanished long ago. When a Smithsonian curator does come upon such an important machine, no one could be more surprised than its owner, who little imagined that the rusting antique in his grandfather's abandoned factory had anything to do with national history. The objects are, of course, original documents in American history, just as surely as any historic archives are. The machine-shop exhibit, among others in the new museum, is itself a capsule chapter written in objects.

In searching beyond the merely curious or especially famous artifacts of history, curators at the Museum of History and Technology have borrowed techniques from their colleagues at the Natural History Museum. One historical "dig" that curators have recently worked is an eighteenth-century Southern plantation whose remains lie buried under a soybean field. Like the Smithsonian's marine bi-

An enticing young woman, the flag, and the spice of danger are deployed, above, in a World War I poster urging Americans to buy war bonds. The Smithsonian's military history collection encompasses posters, maps, uniforms—and weapons such as the nineteenth-century naval cutlass and cutlass-pistol at left.

ologists, the head of the Department of Armed Forces History has been using scuba diving equipment for undersea explorations. He searches for sunken ships, including the renowned Spanish galleons that sank on Caribbean reefs while plying the famed treasure route between Spain and the New World. Sunk with their weapons, furnishings, and cargo, the ships are, as the curator says, "like time capsules." The capsules do not hold up well. In fiction, sunken ships usually lie quietly at the bottom of the ocean, hulls intact, seaweed streaming from the rigging. In fact, after a hundred years in salt water, the waves and the teredo shipworms destroy a ship's exposed timber, leaving coral-encrusted armaments, pottery, and other sturdy artifacts. (Fresh water is kinder. The Smithsonian has on exhibit one of the most splendid of all Revolutionary War relics —the gunboat *Philadelphia* which was sunk at Lake Champlain soon after its launching in 1776 and discovered, well preserved, under sixty-five feet of water in 1935.)

Although it is the grand theme of the "evolution of civilization" that makes the objects on exhibit meaningful at the new museum, the Smithsonian has left little to chance in fulfilling Goode's dream of a museum as a "nursery of living thoughts." The Smith-

sonian has acquired a great deal of expertise in handling exhibits. Displays are worked out from "scripts" written by the curators. Each script spells out a theme to be illustrated, a story to convey the theme, and the objects to be used to make each point in the story. Exhibit designers, following the scripts, work out their productions with painstaking attention to detail. In the Agricultural Hall, for example, the farm machinery and plows rest on a base composed of loose bits of brown cork. It does not look like earth, and is not intended to; but the effect is appropriate. The nineteenth-century machine shop is swabbed several times a year with a mixture of turpentine, linseed oil, and vinegar to maintain an authentic shop aroma. Doubtless, visitors are not keenly aware of these touches; on the other hand, they would surely detect an odor of stale artifice if the curators had not been so meticulous. While some curators prefer to preserve objects in the condition in which they are found, others prefer that visitors see artifacts restored to their original condition. In that way, they believe, the museum can overcome the widespread belief that the past was always shabby and dilapidated. (According to one curator, this prejudice has been so deep seated that, years ago, models of ancient ships were auto-

Ships' figureheads, merry-go-round horses, cigar-store Indians, and other sprightly pieces from the Smithsonian collection of folk art are assembled in a side room, opposite, before being put on display in the new museum.

In the section of musical instruments, a curator works, above, on the restoration of a guitar. At right a bearded young curator tries out a Dulcken harpsichord dating from 1745. Founded by George Brown Goode, the instrument collection is one of the largest in America, ranging from prehistoric bone whistles to exquisitely styled pianos.

matically made tubbier than the ships actually were.) One look at the museum's glisteningly restored automobiles—or, better yet, at one of its sumptuous nineteenth-century coaches—is sure to dispel the prejudice toward the past for all time.

In creating exhibits, the staff can call upon a panoply of ingenious workshops that include specialists in foam rubber, plastics, and photography. The museum's model shop not only builds small-scale working models of mechanical devices but also makes uncanny replicas of objects as well. For one traveling exhibit, the shop turned out a reproduction of a compass used by Lewis and Clark, in which every nick and abrasion was faithfully copied. To duplicate the dry, wrinkled paper on which the compass markings were printed, the shop found an old book and used the paper from the flyleaf. Although the shop does restoration work, it finds itself engaged, too, in the task of aging newly reproduced articles to fill in missing parts of historic relics. Over the years, the staff has acquired a vast fund of techniques for aging everything from leather and brass to felt and linen stitching. To make a wooden fence post look as if it had been weathered for several hundreds of years, they scorch it with a blowtorch and scrape off the charred surface with

a steel brush. The shop is also called upon to make special mannequins for costume displays. By a process of trial and error, the pear shape of a Revolutionary War general was reproduced well enough to fill out the uniform he wore. All of the mannequins at the Smithsonian are modeled to fit the clothes. If the Presidents' wives in the First Ladies Hall look small, it is because they were small. (The faces of the First Ladies, incidentally, are all identical—modeled after a marble bust of Cordelia in the National Collection of Fine Arts. The ladies' hair styles, however, give each of the mannequins a distinctive appearance; the wigs have been styled to duplicate the fashion each First Lady is known to have worn.)

Not all the history and technology specimens the museum has are suitable for exhibition. Nor, indeed, are many of them collected primarily for the purpose of exhibition. Like the other museums at the Smithsonian, the new museum has study collections intended for specialized research and consultation. Its curators, too, publish a large, steady flow of research papers (through the Smithsonian's own editorial offices, whose editors produce enough publications, both learned and popular, to awe even the most imperturbable librarian or bibliophile). Curators' papers not only describe and

A famed ornithologist, the Smithsonian's sixth Secretary, Alexander Wetmore, encouraged studies in history and technology. Above, he accepts a gift for the growing collections. The seventh Secretary, Leonard Carmichael, at right, sought a new home for the collections.

analyze the collections but also detail the research that has gone into making the collections historically meaningful.

One of the Smithsonian's best archives is its collection of model ships representing the development of United States merchant shipping (supplemented by another model collection illustrating the history of naval craft). Though the models are usually built by professional craftsmen, curators ensure their historical accuracy. Where actual plans cannot be found, the historians find other ways of reconstructing authentic models. The model of the pioneer transatlantic steamboat *Savannah*, for example, was built only after a curator pored over old logbooks, customhouse records, and even old Russian newspapers (the *Savannah* crossed the Atlantic and stopped at St. Petersburg in 1819). From these sparse data, and from an immense knowledge of the history of nautical architecture, the curator was able to recreate detailed ship plans for the model builder. The result of such labor is a unique and useful archive. Naval architects laboring over problems in hydrodynamics have often consulted the old ships to discover that more than one modern problem, in propeller design for example, was grappled with long ago. Lately ship designers have consulted the Smithsonian collections for help in

designing catamarans, a type of craft that is now exceedingly popular with weekend sailors. In truth, many old inventions failed simply because they made demands on the technology of their time that could not then be met. Today the ideas are more valuable than ever, and the Museum of History and Technology is the best place to recover them.

The examples of such uses of the collections could be multiplied at length. Historians regularly repair to the Department of Civil History which contains, among other articles, a lithography collection, two thousand non-Currier and Ives prints, and what is thought to be the world's largest collection of keyboard instruments. The Department of Arts and Manufactures contains forty thousand items in its Division of Textiles alone. The Department of Armed Forces History boasts extensive collections from the Hall, Peary, and Byrd Arctic expeditions. And the Department of Science and Technology keeps the records on machines, tools, and the very latest calculating machines.

Even without going backstage into curators' studies and laboratories (to which parts of three floors and the basement of the commodious new museum are devoted), visitors can get some notion of

Immense and unwieldy, relics like the Revolutionary War gunboat, at right, were moved into the new Museum of History and Technology before construction was completed, and the building was built around them. The crisp lines of the finished museum, below, fit well with the architecture of the Federal Triangle in the background.

the range of research in which the museum's historians are engaged.

Exhibits, by-products of historical research, provide some index of the work accomplished since the Department of Arts and Industries was founded. In 1963 a Congressional committee issued a report that outlined exhibits to be installed in the new Museum of History and Technology. The list ran to forty-five items, including a hall of philately (to house one of the most exhaustive stamp collections in the entire world), a hall of numismatics, displays of farm machinery, miniature bridges and tunnels, electrical devices, textiles, rooms devoted to physics, nuclear energy, and medicine—and special historical exhibits such as the "Discovery of America," the "Age of Science," "17th-Century Furnishings," and what is for visitors possibly the most popular exhibit in the entire museum, "Gowns of the First Ladies."

Since the time of Goode, the study of "the evolution of civilization" has come a long way. The novel discipline has found its scholars and interpreters (the museum now has forty permanent members on its research staff); and from the new studies has come what Goode had originally needed—a body of interpretive literature.

The techniques of using museums to excite and educate visitors

—rather than simply to dazzle them with oddities—have come a long way, too, since Goode's time. The old "cabinet technique" of placing assorted curiosities in rows of cases has been rejected; exhibits now tell stories. Objects no longer have brief identifying labels; they are accompanied by several paragraphs of commentary. Visitors who want a guided tour may tote a pocket-size recorder to listen to a running narrative. The jumble is gone, replaced by groupings of choice articles, dramatically lighted and set against the clean, spare lines of the new museum's interior. Goode's concern about the weariness that overtakes museumgoers has been overcome somewhat with escalators. And the new building reaches out to people in a way Goode never dreamed of. Designed with knowledge of the latest fruits of technology, the museum has television cables built right into the walls and a television studio capable of handling a thoroughly professional production. Secretary Langley, for one, would have been pleased. Scattered throughout the museum, near the great flag that flew over Fort McHenry, next to the huge locomotives and the memorabilia of American Presidents, are pairs of drinking fountains—one fountain rigged at adult level, and its companion at a comfortable height for children.

Miniature Mementos
Of Yankee Inventiveness

The diminutive chair above accompanied a patent application submitted by J. H. Belter in the nineteenth century.

An amateur tinkerer, Abraham Lincoln patented the elaborate device above in 1849. Designed to lift boats from sand bars, it was never put to practical use.

Americans have always had a genius for making practical use of abstract theories. And nowhere is the story of Yankee inventiveness illustrated more vividly than in the Smithsonian's selection of nineteenth-century patent models. Exhibited in the various collections of the Museum of History and Technology, these small contrivances were built as working or schematic versions of the latest apparatus of their day, and they astonished contemporaries with the promise of a new, mechanized age. When Thomas Leavitt submitted the model canceling-machine, opposite, in 1879, he made the kind of claim that thrilled a public captivated by efficient gadgets: His invention, he said, could handle fifteen thousand pieces of mail per hour.

The framers of the Constitution had originally endowed Congress with the authority "to promote the Progress of Science and useful Arts, by securing for limited Times to Authors and Inventors the exclusive Right to their respective Writings and Discoveries." And from this terse provision emerged the elaborate patent system that is still in force today. On April 10, 1790, the Patent Office opened its doors for business and promptly announced that it would require each inventor to submit a model, done in miniature or actual size, of the device that he was seeking to patent. So began a flow of mechanical devices from every corner of the country and even from abroad, that in the next century would swell to unmanageable proportions.

By 1823, some eighteen hundred models had been deposited in Washington (seven windmills among them), where they were exhibited in makeshift rooms at the famous Blodgett's Hotel, originally the home of the first theater in the capital. Though a fierce fire burned Blodgett's and all its contents to the ground in 1836, the setback was only temporary. A new building was soon begun, and new models continued to arrive so regularly that within a few years the loss seemed less than catastrophic. "The increase of models," wrote the Commissioner of Patents in 1844, "renders. . .the transaction of business more difficult."

There was another source of congestion that especially vexed the Patent Office. By an odd Congressional whim, the so-called "national cabinet of curiosities" had been crowded into the same building that housed the patent models. Seeking relief, patent officials contacted the Smithsonian. "I have been informed by the Commissioner of Patents," reported Secretary Henry in 1854, "that the space now occupied in the building of the Patent Office by the National Museum, is imperatively required for the display of mod-

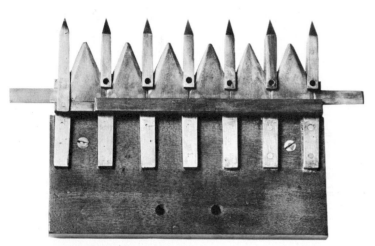

Hussey's cutter bar of 1847, above in a model, established a cutting method that became standard in harvesting grain.

The tiny Selden automobile model above was sent to the Patent Office in 1879. The full-sized car was powered by a six-cylinder internal combustion engine.

els. . . ." And so, three years later, the national collections were packed up and delivered to the Smithsonian, in a move that Henry, for one, judged "mutually beneficial."

The patent models themselves did not come as easily, though. More than half a century would elapse before they found their way into the waiting hands of the Smithsonian staff—and then only because they had become a public scandal. Stimulated by the industrial demands of the Civil War, American inventors increased their output prodigiously, and by 1876 they were sending 14,000 models annually to Washington. "Immediate relief is necessary," declared the Patent Office. Yet, in spite of another fire that destroyed an estimated 76,000 models, the building remained as clogged as ever, as new inventions by the tens of thousands kept streaming in. Eventually the patent law was changed to prohibit inventors from submitting models unless so requested, but by then some 200,000 different objects had accumulated. Exhibiting them, of course, was no longer feasible, and so the models were simply packed away in one empty building after another, piled high in leaky basements and even, at one point, in an abandoned livery stable.

Altogether, more than $200,000 was spent to house and move the models, an expenditure that shocked frugal-minded legislators when at last it came to their attention. In 1908 and 1925, in two sudden spurts of economy, Congress elected to sell off the entire jumbled collection, each time giving the Smithsonian an opportunity first to select and cart away whatever it thought desirable. In the end, about 3,500 models were thus acquired by the Institution, where once again they were put on display so that visitors to Washington could admire the handiwork of American inventors.

Though now preserved in a museum, the patent models have not outlived their usefulness. Occasionally a team of lawyers will descend upon the Smithsonian to see whether or not a model actually works, hoping to prove, or disprove, the validity of a prior patent standing in the way of some new invention. And inventors themselves sometimes come to the Institution to consult the models for hints on how to improve their own devices. Yet, with the passage of time, the patent models have also become useful in a less tangible way. Where once they told tourists what the future had to offer, now they help to illuminate the past, as documents of the technology of their times. And this aim, more than any other, is what the Smithsonian is seeking to promote, to show how America was transformed from a primitive frontier land into a powerful, industrial nation.

Forerunner of the Remington, the Sholes, Glidden, and Soule typewriter of 1868 had one obvious drawback—no provision for anticipating the end of a line.

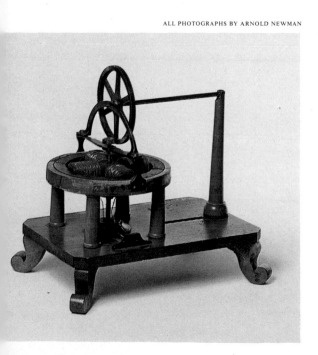

Six hundred locomotives of the last century were built on the principles of the Baldwin Flexible Beam model, above, whose supple running gear permitted engines to negotiate sharp curves.

Applying what he knew of Joseph Henry's work in electromagnetism, Thomas Davenport, in 1837, was the first to patent an electric motor (left).

Treasures of the National Gallery of Art sit for a portrait, at left, with a doorway to another gallery offering a glimpse of three exquisite Vermeer's. Verrocchio's bust of Lorenzo de' Medici, at center, is from the Samuel H. Kress Collection. Rembrandt's magnificent "Self-Portrait," behind Lorenzo, is from the Andrew Mellon Collection. Moving clockwise from da Settignano's bust of a little boy (Andrew Mellon), are Raphael's "St. George and the Dragon" (Andrew Mellon), John Constable's "Wivenhoe Park, Essex" (Widener Collection), "The Small Crucifixion" by Grünewald (Kress), El Greco's "Laocoon" (Kress), David's "Napoleon" (Kress), Gilbert Stuart's portrait of Mrs. Richard Yates (Andrew Mellon), Cézanne's "Still Life" (Chester Dale Collection), Rogier van der Weyden's "Portrait of a Lady" (Andrew Mellon), "A Vase of Flowers" by Jan Davidsz. de Heem acquired through the Andrew Mellon fund, and Houdon's "Diana," a gift of Mrs. Syma Busiel.

PHOTOGRAPH BY ARNOLD NEWMAN

Chapter Five

THE ARTS

The Smithsonian's interest in the arts was not auspiciously begun. Hundreds of Catlin's canvases crowd one another, above, in the Arts and Industries Building at the turn of the century.

Today, works of art have acquired an unimpeachable status at the Smithsonian. Above, a curator from the National Collection of Fine Arts carefully restores a painting by George Catlin. The Smithsonian has some four hundred and fifty works by the famous American artist. Catlin avoided drawing-room portraiture, the vogue for artists in his day, and sought his subjects along America's frontier. He painted the Mandan ritual dancers at right in 1832.

NATIONAL COLLECTION OF FINE ARTS

In 1846, when Congress established the Smithsonian Institution, the legislators provided somewhat vaguely for a "gallery of art" to be formed at the new Institution. The vagueness of the provision was understandable. In the mid-nineteenth century, art galleries were novel ventures in America. The Washington Museum, which had opened in 1836, had a number of paintings among its collections of "between four hundred and five hundred specimens" of various sorts. Only three paintings of that pioneer gallery can now be accounted for: a portrait of Mazarin, a canvas called the "Massacre of the Innocents," and an item titled "Turkish Battle Piece"—all of them by mercifully forgotten artists. Joel Poinsett, the Director of the National Institute, had set up a "department of arts and literature" in 1841, with the resounding sentiment, "Here, the people reign—all power is centered in them . . . no expense or pains should be spared to inspire them with . . . a taste for the fine arts. To this effect, the effort must be made here. It must originate at the seat of Government, and spread from this place over the populous plains and fertile valleys of the land." But in 1846, and for many years thereafter, "a taste for the fine arts" was barely to be found in the plains and fertile valleys of the Republic. As the Smithsoni-

an's Assistant Secretary reported glumly in 1850, "the formation of a gallery of the best paintings is, in this country, almost hopeless."

Americans did not scorn the handiwork of American painters. On the contrary, in the middle of the last century the American painter was perhaps more prosperous and more secure than he has been at any other time. Like a carpenter or cobbler, he was a respected craftsman who frequently enough married off his daughters to the local merchant princes. He had to paint portraits, that was all. As the art critic John Neal wrote in 1829, "You can hardly open the door of a best-room anywhere, without surprizing or being surprized by, the picture of somebody, plastered to the wall and staring at you with both eyes and a bunch of flowers." Yet, as John Walker (the first Chief Curator, and later Director, of the National Gallery of Art) has said, "Until the end of the last century Americans, with rare exceptions, had no time for connoisseurship—for that lust of the eye which, coupled with a sense of possession, leads to the formation of great collections."

Lacking that special lust of the eye, the first curators of the arts began to acquire plaster casts of statues which, it was said, "can be procured very cheap, and convey, of course, a perfect representa-

The British artist William Fisk did Catlin's portrait, at left, in 1849, with the American surrounded by his favorite subjects. Catlin's own painting of a Blackfoot medicine man, above, was done in 1832. Both paintings are now in the custody of the National Collection.

tion of the original." In the 1860's, the Smithsonian gallery had thirty-eight pieces of plaster statuary. Having little money to purchase works of art and no friends with paintings to donate, the Smithsonian did not begin its role in the arts reassuringly.

Nonetheless, to some American painters, the Smithsonian gallery looked hopeful. The Government, it seemed, might become a patron of the arts. After all, the act establishing the Smithsonian had provided for all art belonging to the Government in Washington to be deposited at the Smithsonian. The law had the appearance, at least, of establishing a national gallery of art, and on the strength of that appearance a desperately bankrupt and dauntlessly optimistic American painter named George Catlin was holding off the bailiffs and bill collectors in London. In 1849 Catlin offered for sale to the United States the proudest achievements of his career: six hundred oil paintings of American Indians, at a price of $65,000.

Catlin was one of those American artists who had grown tired of painting portraits of merchants and governors. As a young portraitist in Philadelphia he had had every prospect of a comfortable career until the day he saw some Indian chieftains pass through the city on the way to Washington. "In silent and stoic dignity," he

later recalled, they looked like "lords of the forest." And Catlin fell in love with a three-hundred-year-old philosophical idea: the moral beauty of the Noble Savage. As soon as he could, Catlin left Philadelphia. For six years he traveled through the wild, trackless plains of the West painting his now-famous portraits of noble warriors in their full, doomed glory. When at last he returned to the East, he discovered that his fellow Americans, who had been spending their time fighting the Indians, were not terribly enthralled with his notion of the Noble Savage, and they were certainly not impressed with his crusading lecture on the dignity of the Indian, which he appended to the exhibition of his "Indian Gallery." Reluctantly, in 1839 Catlin made his way to London, still hoping that the United States would recall him and purchase his work en bloc for the sake of the nation. Lionized for a time in London and Paris, by 1849 he had become a poor, eccentric American, deaf and destitute, who unaccountably insisted that his paintings were a national treasure that could not be sold piecemeal. Piecemeal, however, they were put up for security as Catlin went deeper and deeper into debt.

Unfortunately for Catlin, Congress refused to buy his paintings. Then, in 1852 a Philadelphia boilermaker named Joseph Harrison

Two of the pre-eminent masterpieces in the National Gallery (above) are Raphael's "Alba Madonna," at left, and Rembrandt's "The Mill," opposite. Raphael painted the Madonna (now in the Andrew Mellon Collection) about 1510, shortly after he had arrived in Rome and come under the influence of Michelangelo. "The Mill," usually dated about 1650 (and now in the gallery's Widener Collection), is considered to be Rembrandt's finest achievement in landscape painting.

bought up Catlin's IOU's and took possession of the great Indian Gallery. It was a generous gesture, though for some reason Harrison stashed away the paintings in the basement of his boiler factory, where they rested, and in part rotted, for years. In 1879 his widow finally donated the paintings to the place that Catlin had wanted them to go thirty years earlier: the Smithsonian Institution.

By 1879, however, the Smithsonian's gallery of art was only a memory. As late as 1865, it still had not amounted to very much, though with some paintings and plaster statues it continued to appear remotely promising. Then, on the night of January 24, 1865, disaster struck, just as the Smithsonian was fixing up the second-floor gallery to exhibit another collection of Indian paintings, the work of the artist John Mix Stanley. It was a bitterly cold night and the workmen were permitted to bring in a stove to keep themselves warm as they worked. They connected the stovepipe to what they thought was a chimney vent—but the chimney was a ventilating shaft. In a short time the roof of the Smithsonian Building was in flames, and the fire burned to a crisp every one of Stanley's two hundred-odd paintings. For the artist, it was a devastating personal tragedy. For the Smithsonian, it was the end of the art gallery enter-

prise, seemingly for all time. The surviving works of art were loaned out, and the history of art at the Smithsonian came to a dead stop.

The Smithsonian abandoned its gallery at precisely the time that a "craze for art," as some described it, was sweeping the country. During the decades after the Civil War—in "the Gilded Age," as Mark Twain called it—Americans never seemed so rich nor the country so noisy, so raw and disorderly. At the same time, there was a sudden burst of enthusiasm for traveling abroad to buy art. Out of snobbery, out of restlessness, out of a hunger for beauty or status—for a score of different motives—Americans were discovering the delights of culture. American gold, garnered from railways and real estate, steel mills and chain stores, was being showered down upon Europe. The incredibly wealthy, like J. P. Morgan, marched through the Old World like potentates, buying up ten kings' ransoms of porcelains, tapestries, sculptures, and old masters and paying unprecedented prices for them with a cavalier toss of a bank check. Those were the days when it was worth a small fortune to a dealer or an impoverished aristocrat just to be introduced to an American magnate who manifested a taste for the beautiful. When, in 1913, Morgan lay dying in his $500-a-day suite in Rome,

Francesco da Sant' Agata's sculpture of Hercules and Antaeus, above, was done about 1520. It is now in the gallery's Widener Collection.

scores of art dealers, peddlers, collectors, and aristocrats jammed the lobby of his hotel, hoping to make a last sale before the golden spigot would be shut forever.

Morgan was in a class by himself, of course, but other Americans with only a fraction of his wealth were making their contributions to the future museums of America. It was one of these more modest collectors that the Smithsonian had to thank for the revival of art in its domain. The collector's name was Harriet Lane Johnston, niece of the bachelor President James Buchanan and First Lady of the White House during Buchanan's term in office. Like so many Americans of the day, Mrs. Johnston preferred paintings that were remote from American life. But while other Americans purchased the sentimental, bucolic scenes of lowing cattle and misty fields that the French were turning out so deftly for the American market, Mrs. Johnston sought something else. She collected eighteenth-century portraits of lean English aristocrats painted by such masters as Sir Joshua Reynolds and Thomas Gainsborough. When she died, in 1903, Mrs. Johnston bequeathed her collection to the Corcoran Gallery of Art in Washington on condition that it ultimately be delivered to a "national gallery of art," should one ever be established.

Suddenly interest was revived in the Smithsonian's defunct "gallery of art." A national gallery had already been established in Washington, lawyers recalled—at the Smithsonian Institution. The Congressional act of 1846 had named the Institution as the repository for works of art belonging to the Government. Mrs. Johnston's will was taken for interpretation to the Supreme Court of the District of Columbia, and in 1906 the court decided that the Smithsonian did indeed encompass a national gallery and that Mrs. Johnston's paintings should be placed immediately under its care. There was every reason to expect that the new National Gallery of Art would become a great gallery befitting a great nation; a number of gifts followed Mrs. Johnston's bequest, and in 1919 Henry Ward Ranger left a fund of $400,000 to buy art works.

Yet, even before the court had reached its decision on Mrs. Johnston's gift, a far more remarkable collection was offered to the Smithsonian by an unusual Detroit millionaire, Charles Lang Freer. A retired railroad car manufacturer and an ardent collector of American and Oriental art, Freer informed the Smithsonian Regents in 1905 that he was prepared to donate some two thousand works of art, which, as he noted characteristically, have "the power to broad-

The Kress Collection of Renaissance bronzes includes the most distinguished group of reliefs and plaquettes in the world. The portrait of Alberti, at right, the eminent fifteenth-century architect, was probably done by Alberti himself. The medal of Henry IV and Marie de Médicis, below, is considered to be the finest ever done by Guillaume Dupré, foremost of French medalists.

"Death and the Miser," at left, painted by Hieronymus Bosch about 1490, dramatizes a battle between avarice and an angel for a man's soul. The painting is now in the Kress Collection.

en esthetic culture and the grace to elevate the human mind."

Cautiously, the Regents sent a committee to Detroit to examine the unexpected offer. There, in that tough and boisterous Midwestern city, the committee met an exquisitely fastidious and cultivated man, who wore a Vandyke beard and delicate pince-nez. Freer made his guests comfortable, and then, following the courtly customs of Japan, he displayed his cherished works of art—one at a time. Five days later, when the last object had been brought before the Smithsonian committee, Freer was satisfied that they had been given an adequate viewing of his collection.

In truth, the Smithsonian did not immediately snap up Freer's proposal. The committee, in its report to the Regents, referred to his masterpieces as "impressionist art"—a highly suspect style at that time. Then, in December of 1905, President Roosevelt invited the Regents and Mr. Freer to dinner at the White House. The President's interest in having a Freer Gallery was made emphatically clear. Less than a month later, the Smithsonian accepted the gift.

Charles Lang Freer was an exceptionally sensitive and discriminating collector. His first ventures in buying art were indicative of his taste. Eschewing the fashionable landscapes then dominating

NATIONAL GALLERY OF ART

One of only two paintings signed by François Clouet, the portrait of a woman in her bath, at left, is thought to represent Diane de Poitiers, the mistress of Henry II. With the curtains drawn back Diane seems not at all embarrassed; but during the Renaissance, a bath was considered a great luxury, to be savored and shared with companions rather than taken in privacy. The voluptuousness of the surroundings—the rich red curtains, suckling baby, and bowl of fruit—forms a counterpoint to Diane's cool composure. Probably painted about 1571, the portrait is now in the Samuel H. Kress Collection.

the art market, in 1887, at the age of thirty-one, Freer purchased a set of etchings called "Venice, Second Series," by James McNeill Whistler. Freer was taken with Whistler, America's most celebrated expatriate artist—a witty, dandified, Philistine-baiting former West Point cadet who slept in a Chinese bed and scandalized London with his mocking contempt for Victorian ways. And Freer's purchase of "Venice, Second Series" grew into the largest group of the artist's etchings and lithographs in the world. Today the Freer Gallery has a collection of Whistler's works so complete, as one critic has said, that it approaches "a monopoly."

Whistler encouraged Freer's love of Oriental art. The businessman had bought his first Japanese screen paintings in 1892; but they were no more than "skirmish lines of the Oriental advance," Freer later said. With Whistler as a friend and mentor, Freer's interest in Oriental art grew to a devoted quest for Chinese bronzes, jades, and porcelains, for Persian manuscripts, and for the paintings and sculpture of India, Egypt, and Syria. In 1900 the 48-year-old bachelor millionaire retired from business and, until his death in 1919, concentrated on expanding and studying his collections. He did not pretend to scholarship, but he became an astute judge

of the treasures of the East. Although Freer never lived to see his gallery completed and opened in 1923, the gallery represents all the qualities he himself loved. Uncluttered, serene, and self-contained, it is a place of eminent reticence and refinement. It accepts no gifts of objects for the collections proper and makes no loans. Its purchases are made slowly and thoughtfully; its exhibits change slowly, as Freer himself had decreed. The gallery's collections have been expanded so that they now contain ceramics representative of the pottery traditions of the Near and Far East. The Freer's medieval Armenian manuscripts comprise one of the two finest groups in America. And, of course, its Chinese paintings and ceremonial bronzes, Japanese paintings and sculpture, and Persian and Indian miniatures are among the most important collections of their kind ever assembled. For students of Oriental art, the Freer Gallery is a world-renowned pilgrimage center and a thriving home for scholarly research, the only establishment of its kind in the world—a lovely, unchanging gem in the ever-changing Smithsonian.

By the time the Freer Gallery was opened, the National Gallery of Art had more than doubled in size. At first its paintings were jammed into a room of the Arts and Industries Building, but in

The tranquil beach at Etretat, above, was painted by Gustave Courbet about 1869.

The ballerina Mlle. Malo was painted off stage by Degas in about 1877.

1910 the gallery was allotted space in the north hall of the Museum of Natural History. It would remain there "temporarily," the Smithsonian *Annual Report* said that year. Without a building of its own, the National Gallery of Art was almost doomed in its first decades. By 1920 there was no space to hang new paintings, and, as a consequence, very few donors appeared. Ironically enough, it was in that same year that the National Gallery became a full-fledged bureau of the Smithsonian, with William H. Holmes, a Smithsonian anthropologist (and a painter in his own right), serving as its first director. Throughout the 1920's, Holmes did his best to get money for a building. But the National Gallery was beginning to seem a very ill-starred venture indeed. Holmes tried to appeal to the public's pride, to its patriotism, and even to its love of a good investment. The National Gallery of Art, he calculated in more than one magazine article, had been receiving, until 1920, $500,000 worth of gifts a year. Since 1920 the figure had dropped as low as $40,000 a year. By attracting valuable gifts again, a spacious art museum would easily pay for itself many times over.

Whether as art or as business, the National Gallery was not appealing very strongly to many people. As Holmes ruefully reported in 1926, the gallery was "practically dormant." Yet, in those moribund years, the oddest of personal circumstances did bring a significant donation to the gallery. It came from one John Gellatly of New York and included among a large number of art objects a fine collection of American paintings, notably seventeen works by Albert Pinkham Ryder, the eccentric hermit who lived in squalor in New York and painted brooding apocalyptic works as memorable as anything ever done by an American. The circumstances of Gellatly's gift to the Smithsonian were novel. A wealthy widower in his middle seventies, Gellatly intended to marry a woman nearly a half century younger than he. Suspecting that his fiancée's motives for accepting might not be entirely romantic, he went to Europe in 1928—still unbetrothed—and spent his fortune on art works which he then bestowed on the Smithsonian Institution. In 1931, a year after he was married, Gellatly died, quite penurious by millionaire standards, much to the chagrin of his widow.

About the time that Gellatly was unburdening himself of his wealth, another art buyer was pondering the dismaying condition of art in the nation's capital. His name was Andrew Mellon, Secretary of the Treasury and member of the Smithsonian Art Commis-

CONTINUED ON PAGE 106

Andrew W. Mellon: Acquiring a Taste for the Finest

It is "the greatest collection ever assembled by private hands," exclaimed one New York critic in 1937. And Lord Duveen, never one to mince superlatives, described Andrew Mellon's art collection as "the finest in the universe." Indeed, "Uncle Andy," as Warren Harding liked to call Andrew Mellon behind his back, had outdistanced all his fellow multi-millionaires in acquiring art. Yet if his collection was indisputably the best, it was by no means the biggest. Whereas J. P. Morgan left well in excess of 10,000 objects, Mellon gave the nation just 115 pictures (exclusive of American portraits). Always a stern advocate of governmental economy, he spent millions on his paintings but never wasted a penny. Quality was what he sought, not quantity. "He was princely," noted an admirer, "but not prodigal."

Such selectivity was in keeping with a refined, highly disciplined personality. Frail and ascetic-looking, as in Oswald Birley's portrait opposite, he wore dark, quietly luxurious clothes and spoke infrequently. There was a patrician aura of assuredness about him. A fastidious connoisseur of food and wine, he once kept the Premier of France waiting on the telephone while he finished with his breakfast. Men like Frick and Carnegie were new to wealth, but the Mellon bank went back a generation, enough to guarantee prestige without the need for ostentation. Even during his years as Secretary of the Treasury, he remained a retiring, silently powerful figure.

In art, as in everything else, he knew exactly what he liked. Sculpture, nudes, and contemporary paintings were not to his taste, nor were pictures with dark backgrounds, or ones that showed unpleasant or harrowing scenes. A picture had to please him, and a famous name was not enough. Once he turned down a fine Raphael portrait simply because he did not care for it, even though he owned no Raphaels at the time. Partial to Dutch landscapes and English portraiture, he hung the walls of his Washington apartment with Hals and Hobbema, Raeburn and Lawrence, and placed a Turner landscape above the mantelpiece. At one point Lord Duveen leased the apartment below, moved in "some beautiful things" to offer to his favorite client, and left the key with Mellon. There, at night, the solitary old man, clad in dressing gown and slippers, would spend hours pondering the unfamiliar canvases about him.

Yet, however pronounced his own preferences, Mellon could suppress them in the interests of a larger plan. It was one thing, he knew, to buy for his home, but quite a different matter to build a great museum. After 1927, when he first determined to found a National Gallery, he began to make purchases less to gratify his personal taste than to represent the greatest schools and periods of Western art. Titian's voluptuous "Venus with a Mirror," for example, was altogether too indecorous for him to hang in his home, but he bought it from the Hermitage nonetheless because it filled a gap in his projected gallery. Some years later, shopping for a Giorgione, he was prepared to take an "Adoration of the Shepherds" from Duveen until he learned that Bernard Berenson would not certify it as a Giorgione, considering it instead a Titian. "I don't want another Titian," Mellon snapped. "Find me a Giorgione."

It was wholly characteristic of the man, whose sense of propriety was so keen, to refuse to put his name on the museum that he founded. What he wanted, after all, was a National Gallery, not a monument to himself. His one condition was that future acquisitions match the quality of his own collection. And by so stipulating, this self-effacing man stamped the gallery with a personal imprint far more meaningful than his name—with that same exacting standard of excellence that made him the outstanding collector of his day.

Charles Lang Freer, founder of the Smithsonian's gallery of Oriental and American art, was painted, at right, by his friend Whistler. Freer did not confine his collecting to Japan and China; the brilliant golden goat at left comes from Persia and dates from the sixth or fifth century B.C. The museum, photographed below from its interior court, is visited by Orientalists from all over the world as well as by casual museum visitors.

ALL: FREER GALLERY OF ART

CONTINUED FROM PAGE 103

sion. A taciturn, unassuming man (when his name was given to President Harding to consider for the job of Secretary of the Treasury, Harding said, "I never heard of him."), Mellon did not say much about his own plans; but then again, he hardly ever spoke at all. What spoke for him, albeit as discreetly as circumstances would allow, was the singular fact that Mellon was worth more than $500,000,000. If there was to be a truly great national art museum in Washington, Mellon decided, he himself was going to create it. His idea of greatness was lordly, as befitted a man of such staggering resources. What America required, he believed, was not just fine art, not merely the work of Europe's old masters, but nothing less than the greatest works that the greatest old masters of Europe had ever produced.

Mellon's collecting began rather modestly. On his frequent trips to Europe with Henry Clay Frick (who later established the Frick Collection in New York), Mellon made small purchases, of several thousand dollars apiece, of seventeenth-century Dutch and eighteenth-century English paintings. But, as his fervor for collecting grew, and his highly personal tastes developed, Mellon entered a league all his own in the art market. A half million dollars (the

The painting of a Mongol leading a horse, above, dates from the Yüan dynasty, the period when Kublai Khan and his "barbarian" warriors dominated China.

price he paid for a Rembrandt "Self-Portrait" and Holbein the Younger's portrait of Edward VI) became a rock-bottom price for the alert banker. Old masters were growing scarce by 1930, but working in the dark secrecy that great art collectors thrive on (Mellon's fellow collector Joseph Widener once remarked that if people knew what was spent on a painting "it might foster a spirit of Bolshevism"), Mellon proceeded to carry off one of the most remarkable art-buying coups of all time—from the Bolsheviks. Russia's commissars were hard pressed for cash to pay off some loans. A shrewd young German dealer learned of their willingness to sell some of the masterpieces in Leningrad's Hermitage Gallery and got in touch with Knoedler's, one of Mellon's dealers. Mellon purchased, sight unseen, twenty-one of the Hermitage paintings, including such supreme masterpieces as Raphael's "Alba Madonna" (for which he paid $1,166,000), Botticelli's "Adoration of the Magi" (for a price of $838,350), Raphael's "St. George and the Dragon" (at a cost of nearly $750,000), and Jan van Eyck's "Annunciation" (for more than $500,000). Prices, of course, do not begin to tell the story of the value of such works of art. Van Eyck, for example, is generally considered the discoverer of oil painting, the first man to use linseed oil as a medium for color. Though van Eyck's position as the pioneer in oils has been disputed, John Walker has pointed out: "Certainly he was the first to achieve a naturalistic rendering of interior space, or in less technical terms, the effect of looking through an open window or door into a room." Raphael's "Alba Madonna," aside from its exceptional, tender beauty, is one of the finest technical achievements in Renaissance painting (if the compositional elements in a round painting are not in perfect harmony, the picture will appear to roll like a wheel). And Botticelli's "Adoration of the Magi" represents one of the finest paintings to come from the late-fifteenth-century Florence of Lorenzo de' Medici. The Hermitage purchase brought Mellon other superb masterpieces too: the "Study for Innocent X," by Velázquez, Perugino's "Crucifixion with Saints," Titian's "Venus with a Mirror," Veronese's "Finding of Moses," and a number of works by van Dyck and Franz Hals.

When a man like Mellon entered the art market, rival collectors could do nothing but sit by and watch, while art dealers prayed for a chance to collect commissions. One of Mellon's sources for art works was a spectacular super-salesman by the name of Joseph Duveen, who made a specialty of buying up old masters. Using ser-

Gilbert Stuart, a leading portraitist of the eighteenth and nineteenth centuries, is represented in the National Collection of Fine Arts by the portrait above of young Stephen Decatur.

vants as his spies, he learned when an art-rich but cash-poor nobleman was ready to sell the ancestral treasures, and would buy the works on multi-million-dollar speculations, holding them until, by dint of painstaking diplomacy, he could bring an American Croesus to the point of a sale. Run-of-the-mill old masters Duveen looked on with utmost contempt, and small-fry millionaires he would have nothing to do with. To the flamboyant Duveen, Mellon seemed excruciatingly cautious and unbearably sphinxlike. But gradually, a few at a time, Mellon increased his little collection of the world's greatest masterpieces. By the end of 1937, he had spent about $30,000,000 to acquire some 115 works of art from the hands of such titans as van Eyck, Holbein, Titian, Rubens, and Rembrandt. In December of 1936, he had written a letter to the President announcing the largest gift an individual had ever given to a government, and one of the most awesome gifts anyone had ever given to anybody. Mellon offered his entire collection to the United States, along with $15,000,000 to erect a suitable building and $5,000,000 more as an endowment fund. Mellon's conditions were that this great offering be called the National Gallery of Art and that it be placed under the protection of the Smithsonian Insti-

The marble "Greek Slave," above, done in 1843 by Hiram Powers, was the most celebrated sculpture of its day.

Albert Pinkham Ryder's tempestuous "The Flying Dutchman," at left, was first exhibited in 1887. Much of Ryder's inspiration was drawn from poets like Chaucer, Shakespeare, Byron, and Poe. This canvas, one of the artist's most highly regarded works, was inspired by Wagner's opera of the same name. Abbott Thayer, a contemporary of Ryder, did the sketch of his daughter Mary, above, in the 1880's. Both painters were romantics. Ryder saw violent emotions personified in nature; Thayer saw a gentleness and innocence in nature and in women. The two works here are now in the National Collection of Fine Arts.

tution as an independent bureau with its own board of trustees. A few months after Congress formally accepted the gift—and the conditions—Mellon died, at the age of eighty-two. He was never to see the immense National Gallery—one of the largest marble structures in the world—that now stands so regally on the Mall.

But if Mellon's collection now constituted the National Gallery of Art, what was the establishment recognized by the Court in 1906 as the National Gallery of Art? The answer is that Mrs. Johnston's collection, and the collections that had been joined to it, were renamed the National Collection of Fine Arts. More was intended than a change of names, for in truth not everyone in Congress was delighted with Mellon's gift. During the debate over the terms of Mellon's National Gallery, a forceful minority of Senators led by Robert La Follette was concerned that a national gallery of masterpieces would not encourage modern art and American artists. Although the various amendments these Senators proposed for the National Gallery bill were voted down, Congress in the next year sketched a new and imposing role for the National Collection of Fine Arts. It was to serve as an agency for widening American appreciation of art and for encouraging American artists. This was a

mission born at a favorable moment in America's history—during the height of the New Deal era, a time when the Work Projects Administration had put thousands of jobless artists, writers, actors, and designers to work to bring art exhibits, plays, and concerts to thousands of hamlets in America. As Congress saw it, the National Collection of Fine Arts was to join in that new and radical enterprise of sinking the roots of American art deeper into American soil.

And yet, despite its demanding standards (and the astronomical costs of meeting them) it was the National Gallery of Art that thrived and the National Collection of Fine Arts, despite its new, dynamic mission, that remained dormant for many years. In 1937, when ground was broken for the National Gallery building, Mellon's total gift of 132 paintings (he had added the works of several classic American portraitists at the end of his life) would scarcely have been able to fill the more than three and one-half acres of gallery area. As Mellon's friend David Finley, the first director of the gallery, said, there were barely enough works of art "to decorate a good-sized duplex apartment." It took only four other gifts to fill out the museum; the gifts were, to be sure, magnanimous.

In the 1930's Andrew Mellon had spoken of his plan for a na-

tional gallery with Joseph Widener. Widener was not quick to offer his collection for such a museum, but, shortly after construction of the gallery began, David Finley visited with Widener and persuaded him to donate his works of art to the museum. The Widener Collection had been begun by Joseph's father, Peter A. B. Widener, and it would have made a splendid museum of its own. It included, for example, such treasures as Vermeer's "A Woman Weighing Gold" and "Young Girl with a Flute," Titian's "Venus and Adonis," and an extraordinary collection of fourteen canvases by Rembrandt. Among the Rembrandt paintings was "The Mill," which, as the English critic Roger Fry has said, "is surely the most complete expression of the dramatic mood in landscape that has ever been achieved in Western art." According to the nineteenth-century painter John Constable, the single painting is, by itself, "sufficient to form an epoch in the art" of landscapes.

In 1938 David Finley made a visit to Samuel Kress, the five-and-ten-cent store king. Kress, too, thought he might build a museum of his own. Finley arrived at Kress's home one day at three o'clock in the afternoon and left at ten o'clock in the evening, with a promise that Kress would donate his works of art to the National Gal-

lery. Kress had only begun his collecting in the early 1920's, and he made his greatest purchases from 1937 until his death in 1945. Thereafter, the Kress Foundation, headed by Samuel Kress's brother, Rush, spent more than thirty million dollars to complete the collection. The connoisseurs at the National Gallery guided Rush Kress in his purchases, and the gallery obtained the famous "Adoration of the Magi" by Fra Angelico and Fra Filippo Lippi, Botticelli's portrait of Giuliano de' Medici, Bellini's "Portrait of a Condottiere," and hundreds of other paintings—"items" as Samuel Kress called them—that make up the most complete collection of Italian Renaissance art in the world.

The third outstanding donation to follow Mellon's gift was the Lessing J. Rosenwald Collection, presented to the gallery in 1943. Brought together with masterful discrimination, it consists of more than seventeen thousand woodcuts, drawings, lithographs, etchings, and prints of various sorts. Collections of prints frequently comprise many more works than Rosenwald has gathered; but perhaps no other collection has been assembled with such selectivity.

The museum's latest major collection, donated by Chester Dale, is dedicated, primarily, to showing the most brilliant works of

Washington's old Patent Office building, above in a nineteenth-century engraving, was recently set aside to house both the National Collection of Fine Arts and the National Portrait Gallery. Combined, the two art galleries form a center for studies of American art and American history. Winslow Homer's water color of bear hunters, at left, is taken from the National Collection's group of nineteenth-century American paintings. The two caricatures at right, part of the new Portrait Gallery's collections, give irreverent impressions of two Americans—the dapper author Bret Harte, and the absent-minded journalist Horace Greeley.

Bret Harte, by Sir Leslie Ward, 1879

Horace Greeley, by Thomas Nast, 1872

French art in the past century and a half. Dale was shrewd enough to become a partner of an art dealer—the Galerie Georges Petit—which specialized in impressionist and postimpressionist canvases. As a result, Chester Dale (with the help of his wife Maud) assembled one of the finest collections anywhere of French paintings of the nineteenth and twentieth centuries, including such outstanding works as Manet's "Old Musician" (the artist's most ambitious work in terms of the complexity of its composition), Renoir's "A Girl with a Watering Can" (one of the gallery's most popular paintings), and Gauguin's "Fatata te Miti," painted only a few months after the artist first arrived in Tahiti.

Taken together, these five major collections, along with many other individual donations, form a gallery with a standard of excellence easily equal to any museum in the world—and it was created in the breathtakingly short span of twenty-five years.

In the years the National Gallery was being formed, the National Collection of Fine Arts was overshadowed by the astounding munificence of men like Mellon. Re-formed at a time when Americans were eager to encourage native art, it passed through many lean years nonetheless. But recently the National Collection has been springing back to active life. In 1953, for example, a report submitted by the Commission of Fine Arts to President Eisenhower called for the restoring of American art to "a healthy relationship to the life of the community"; and, as a first step toward achieving that relationship, the Smithsonian Institution Traveling Exhibition Service was set up as an office of the National Collection of Fine Arts. The Traveling Exhibition Service immediately began serving as a self-supporting agency for distributing art (and other) exhibitions to museums and institutions around the country. Finally, in 1958, Congress set aside Washington's old Patent Office building as an art gallery. Today, the National Collection of Fine Arts, homeless since 1906 (one could say since 1846), has found a home. By 1967 it will be ready to exhibit collections in the old Patent Office building that will survey American and contemporary art on a broad scale: not only fine art, but the entire field of the plastic arts in America, including decorative arts and design. Just as importantly, the National Collection of Fine Arts is now laying plans to fulfill the mission set out before it a quarter of a century ago—to encourage the growth of art in America. Recently it launched a series of major exhibits of American art, celebrating such native painters as Stuart

Ætatis suæ 21. Aᵒ. 1616.

Matoaks als Rebecka daughter to the mighty Prince Powhatan Emperour of Attanoughkomouck als Virginia converted and baptized in the Christian faith, and Wife to the worᵗ Mʳ Tho: Rolff.

Copley's portrait of Henry Laurens (above), a Revolutionary statesman, was left to the Portrait Gallery by Andrew Mellon.

Rebecca Rolfe (opposite), better known as Pocahontas, was painted by an unknown artist in 1616, a year before her death in England. A gift of Andrew Mellon, the canvas is one of the most highly cherished possessions of the new Portrait Gallery.

A third Andrew Mellon gift to the Portrait Gallery, the bold impression of Andrew Jackson on a battlefield, above, is unsigned, but attributed to Ralph E. W. Earl.

Davis and George Catlin. To make American art more widely available, it is planning to bring art exhibits (possibly in the form of "artmobiles") to remote schools and hamlets and to help communities set up their own local art centers. It hopes, too, to stimulate native talent by setting up a scholarship program for promising contemporary artists and by establishing a center for the study of historic American art.

In the refurbished old Patent Office building, the National Collection will have a full-fledged partner. In 1962 Congress established as a bureau of the Smithsonian another art and history enterprise that had long been conspicuously lacking in America: a national portrait gallery of notable Americans. Although the subject of the painting is more important than the painter's ability to the Portrait Gallery, the new bureau begins life with a sizable advantage: a gift of some thirty-five portraits painted by such great eighteenth-century American masters as C. W. Peale and John Singleton Copley. They were purchased by Andrew Mellon years ago and were set aside by him for the day when a national portrait gallery would finally be established. The new bureau is, most emphatically, not only a pantheon of great heroes. It is designed to include all people

who have made a real contribution to American history, whether they were beloved or detested, hero or villain. The main criterion is that they be named in the comprehensive *Dictionary of American Biography* (which includes Aaron Burr as well as Alexander Hamilton). The only hitch here, perhaps, is that the National Portrait Gallery will have to find generous citizens with a real interest in history, for the gallery must now depend entirely on private gifts for its collection. Besides its permanent portrait exhibition, the National Portrait Gallery will also establish a study center which it hopes will be of increasing service to students of American history. The center will contain a vast archival record of available likenesses —be they paintings, coins, rough sketches, or death masks—of every person who figured in the development of America.

In all, the complex of the four art galleries at the Smithsonian comprises one of the most eminent of all the world's great collections of art. If there are "two cultures" of art and science at war, there is no sign of it at the Smithsonian Institution. It commodiously embraces both fields of endeavor, and never more actively than today, one hundred years after the Smithsonian's seedling of art almost burned to a crisp.

Ancient Art
From the Orient

The bronze vessel above, of the Fang i type, dates from the Chou dynasty, one of China's most splendid eras.

"There is at this place a very fine marble Palace," wrote Marco Polo of his visit to Chandu, "the rooms of which are gilt and painted with figures of men and beasts and birds . . . all executed with such exquisite art that you regard them with delight and astonishment." For nearly six centuries, Western minds were fired by such marvelous accounts, mixtures of fact and fantasy, that enveloped the isolated East in exotic mystery. During the seventeenth century millions of Chinese porcelains reached Europe; and the eighteenth century became the great age of *chinoiserie*. Then, in 1853, Commodore Perry and his "black ships" sailed into Tokyo Bay and opened up Japan to foreign trade. Within a few years, connoisseurs of art in Paris had discovered that the packages of tea arriving from "the Secret Empire" were wrapped in colored prints, valued little more than newspapers by exporters in Japan. The late nineteenth-century passion for collecting Oriental art had begun in earnest.

Charles Lang Freer, founder of the Freer Gallery of Art, was very much a part of this romantic movement. Like the wistful aristocrat in Boston who named his yacht "Nirvana," Freer felt oppressed by the turbulent commercial world of his day, and sought repose in such serene artistic images as the graceful, thirteenth-century Chinese Bodhisattva opposite. Yet, romantic as he was, this sensitive millionaire from Detroit was seeking something less fantastic than the magic carpet ride to "the flowery land" that so enthralled most of his contemporaries. At a time when American homes were cluttered with Japanese metalware from Tiffany's, peacock feathers and parasols, and Oriental prints of dubious authenticity, Freer became convinced that he was being deceived, and embarked upon a pilgrimage to the Orient to discover for himself what was genuine. Applying a "fine-tooth comb," he cast aside "some of the most beautiful fakes you have ever seen," and even then could not be pleased. His early Japanese paintings, he soon decided, were really based on an earlier, more refined tradition. Journeying to the caves of Lungmen, in interior China, recently studied by French scholars, he was able to help show the world that fine examples of early Chinese art still survived, unknown to the Western world.

"We have but scratched the surface," Freer later admitted to a friend. Still, he did make certain that others after him would carry on what he had just begun. The Freer Gallery of Art, opened in 1923, was designed as more than a public museum. From the outset, it undertook a program of intensive, scholarly research, dig-

A Bodhisattva, or Buddha-to-be, is represented above in a Japanese sculpture, done in wood, of the Suiko period.

ging deeper where its founder had intuitively pointed out the way.

Even today, the main task of scholars at the Freer is to describe, date, and analyze the contents of their collections, which include such varied items from the East as bronzes, paintings, sculptures, potteries, lacquers, manuscripts, and porcelains. Any single object among the ten thousand that the gallery owns may pose the most perplexing riddles, calling for an intimate understanding of the culture that produced it. There is one bronze mirror at the Freer, for example, that has a decorated knob on its back, representing a tortoise and serpent entwined. What is the meaning of this image? When and where was the mirror made? Like a sleuth on the track of elusive clues, Dr. John A. Pope, presently Director of the Freer, pieced together a tentative solution. The tortoise and serpent, he knew, symbolized the Dark Warrior of the North, who in Taoist lore controls the mystical force called Yin, the dark opponent of Yang. That would explain why the tortoise-serpent image appeared on the dark side of the mirror, opposite the bright reflecting surface. Moving on, Pope then pointed out that the mirror, because of its style, doubtless came from a place called Shōu-chou, which, just after the middle of the second century B.C., had become a center for cosmological speculation by the leading Taoist philosophers of the day, heirs to the tradition of the great Chinese sage Lao-tzu. "It does not seem at all inappropriate," Pope cautiously concluded, "that this mirror should spring from that time, that place, and that body of thought."

Put together, such bits and pieces of scholarship can, in the end, speak eloquently of an entire civilization. Among the many programs of research currently in progress at the Freer, there is one devoted to a very early set of Chinese bronzes, some of which are remnants of the Shang dynasty, a royal line of the second millennium B.C. Some thirty-five years ago, historians in the West dismissed the Shang period, mentioned prominently in Chinese history, as mythological fantasy. Then, much as Heinrich Schliemann startled the world by unearthing the remains of Homeric Troy, Chinese scholars dug up the last Shang capital, at Anyang in the valley of the Yellow River. Thus the prized collection of Shang bronzes at the Freer has taken on a new significance. Their advanced technique and decorative ingenuity now are telling evidence of a splendid age that for centuries was buried from the view of historians.

Truth can be strange, indeed. At the Freer, as Marco Polo said centuries ago in introducing his famous book, there are "all kinds of wonderful things"—far more than Marco Polo ever dreamed.

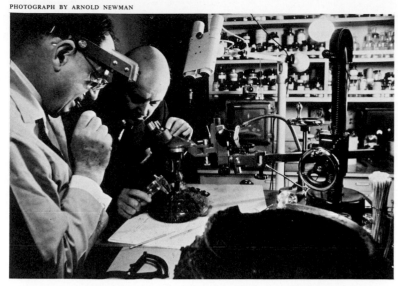

Above, John A. Pope, Director of the Freer, and to his right, Rutherford J. Gettens, head of the Technical Laboratory, scrutinize a Chinese bronze of the Chou dynasty.

After ousting the ancient Shang dynasty, the house of Chou ruled China for nearly one thousand years, until 256 B.C. The bronze ceremonial vessel below, cast in the shape of an elephant, dates from the early Chou period, a time of cultural transition. The one above is late Chou, a troubled age of ferment that left the world the wisdom of Confucius and Lao-tzu.

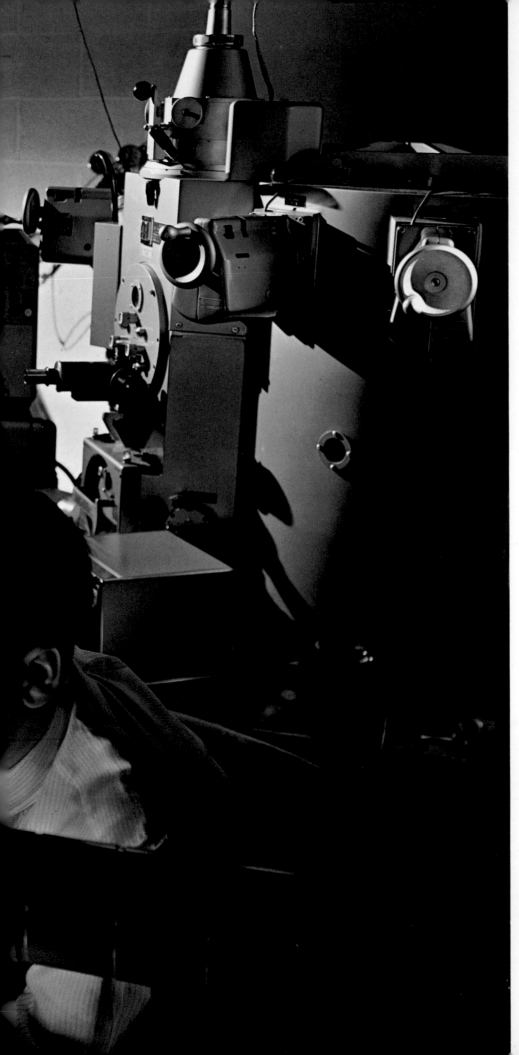

Chapter Six

THE
SOCIETY
OF
SCHOLARS

119

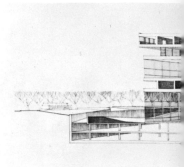

A model of a blue whale is placed in the natural history museum's Hall of the Sea—one of many new, modern exhibit halls.

Two new Smithsonian buildings are in the planning stages: the National Air and Space Museum (above, in an architect's drawing) and the John F. Kennedy Center for the Performing Arts (at right in a model). The drawing of the Air and Space Museum, designed by Gyo Obata, reveals a spacious interior that will accommodate giant rocket displays—and fifty thousand visitors a day. The Kennedy Center was designed by the architect Edward Durrell Stone.

Today, the Smithsonian Institution is well into its second century of life. Two hundred years have passed since the birth of its enigmatic founder, James Smithson. Almost a century has passed since the death of its first Secretary and guiding spirit, Joseph Henry. By the time-scale of American science, it is an old and hallowed institution. Yet the Smithsonian has not slipped into a peaceful and eventless old age. The unparalleled growth and complexity of contemporary society have created a host of new opportunities and responsibilities "for the increase and diffusion of knowledge among men"—the Smithsonian's original mandate. With substantial support from public and private sources, the Institution is vigorously engaged in the Herculean task of updating and improving all of its scholarly and public services.

The most obvious signs of this inner ferment are the buildings: the new Museum of History and Technology; the new wings added to the Museum of Natural History; the expanded facilities for the Oceanographic Sorting Center at the old Naval Weapons Plant; the ten-year program of capital improvements now begun at the National Zoological Park; the remodeling of the neoclassic old Patent Office building as a new home for the National Collection of

Fine Arts and the National Portrait Gallery; and a new wing on the Astrophysical Observatory's offices in Cambridge, Massachusetts. The interior of the old Smithsonian building is being restored in its original mid-nineteenth century style, in homage to those first scholars whose thoughtful precepts have informed the entire history and progress of the Institution. For the Mall itself, numerous projects are designed to enliven its solemn formality and to give some sense of community to the monumental structures marshaled on either side of its long straight sward: music from the tower of the Smithsonian Building; one or more sculpture gardens; outdoor exhibits discreetly placed to orient the visitor toward the experiences awaiting him within; and café tables, refreshments, and band and symphony concerts on the terrace of the Museum of History and Technology.

At the same time, a number of new projects that are taking shape will be major additions to the diverse public activities of the Institution. On the shore of the Potomac near the Lincoln Memorial, the ground has been broken for a new Smithsonian bureau: the John F. Kennedy Center for the Performing Arts. Originally known as the National Cultural Center when it was first authorized in

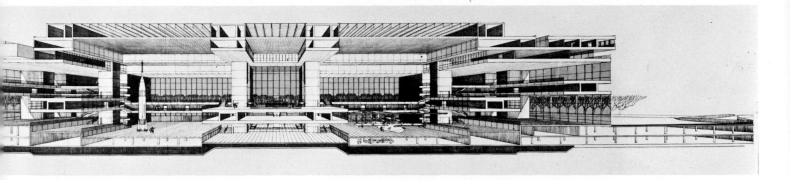

PHOTOGRAPH BY LOUIS CHECKMAN

1958, it was designated in 1964 as the sole official Washington memorial to the late President, who during his term of office had been instrumental in making the center possible. As a national home for the performing arts, the center will contain a concert hall, an opera and ballet house, a theater, and a small film auditorium. The Smithsonian is also making plans for possible daytime uses of the center for lectures, art exhibitions, demonstrations, and experiments with new audio-visual techniques designed to give a sense of direct participation in history, science, and the arts.

The unparalleled collections of the National Air and Space Museum have for years been dispersed, some in the Arts and Industries Building, others in the "temporary" (World War I) hangar-like structure next door, and the largest part in warehouses. It is now planned that by 1969 the Museum will come into its own on the Mall in a new building of contemporary design befitting its subject: the grand leap of man, the earthling, into the hostile environments of air and space. Equipped with lofty exhibit areas large enough to accommodate giant rockets, and a futuristic complex of mezzanines and galleries for detailed teaching exhibits, the museum will be far more than a repository of historic craft and memorabilia. Supple-

menting the broad exhibition that traces the development of flight, the museum hopes to prepare its visitors for an understanding of the future. Exhibits will show the basic scientific principles of flight and rocketry and will illuminate the supporting contributions made to the great enterprise by such allied fields as physics, mathematics, metallurgy, astrophysics, and space medicine. Stripping away the mystery from, say, some future flight to Mars, the new museum will give the visitor an understanding of how it was accomplished and of the enormous depth and scope of the achievement. For flight has been the work of thousands of men, with countless illuminating failures and dead-end efforts, and these, too, the museum will show. Other exhibits will explore the problems that continue to face us in the strange new environment beyond the earth; novel conditions such as weightlessness, meteoroid hazards, and solar radiation. With the help of flexible exhibits, the museum will keep abreast of the latest developments in space to create a museum as scholarly as a history text and as fresh as a newspaper headline.

A radically different kind of Smithsonian museum is being planned, too. Known as the National Armed Forces Museum, it was authorized by Congress in 1961 to "commemorate and display the contri-

Above, at the Smithsonian's new Oceanographic Sorting Center, specimens are packed in jars or sealed in plastic bags for distribution to specialists. Among its other duties, the center organizes data for marine ecologists and biogeographers. Opposite, at the Smithsonian Astrophysical Observatory, a researcher at the control console of the CDC 3200 computer feeds in tracking data on artificial satellites for one of the observatory's research programs.

A researcher in the Radiation Laboratory (left) checks the progress of an experiment in the marine biology lab.

butions made by the military forces of the Nation, toward creating, developing, and maintaining a free, peaceful, and independent society and culture in the United States of America." As presently conceived, the new museum will have no walls; it will be set instead in a great parkland area near the nation's capital, stretching over a varied terrain of forest, fields, hills, and shoreline. Historic fortifications, trenches, gun batteries, and earthworks and campsites will be set down exactly as they appeared in various conflicts of the past. Thus, on what amounts to a simulated field of battle, the museum will trace the technological evolution of warfare. The museum will emphasize, too, the peacetime role of the military in the development of American science and technology, a role the military has played since the days when the Army Engineers built, singlehandedly, many of America's roads, bridges, and harbors.

And yet this catalogue of bricks and mortar, of bureaus and museums, is but a superficial index of the central purposes of the Institution. While the public education functions of the museum exhibits are extremely important, the largest part of the Smithsonian's inventory is its research collections rarely seen by the public. At the Smithsonian, museums are scholarly workshops, not warehouses.

From the beginning, a major objective of Smithsonian scholarship has been to support original research for the sake of knowledge itself, rather than for its practical economic consequences, and to promote new lines of inquiry not being pursued elsewhere. However, in the days of Secretary Henry, organized knowledge, as it exists today, was uncharted territory. For many years, the choice of fields such as solar radiation or American ethnology was frequently based on the particular bent of individual Smithsonian scholars. Now the world of learning has been extensively traveled, subdivided, and, in some areas, overpopulated. The intervention of massive Government support has given disproportionate emphasis to science, and within science to certain specialties such as atomic energy and medical research. While enormous amounts of money go into some fields, others, shorn of support and prestige, are threatened with extinction, the victims of changing national needs and changeable intellectual fashions. It is in this context that the present Secretary of the Smithsonian Institution, S. Dillon Ripley, has shaped the general principles of Smithsonian scholarship into a concerted policy to "bolster the unfashionable" branches of learning, and to help, where possible, to achieve a balanced development of the scholarly domain.

After years of nominal support, the Institution is giving increasing attention to history and art. The professional staff research facilities, and publication programs devoted to these fields, have been greatly enlarged. The new series of publications—*Contributions from the Museum of History and Technology*—is receiving enthusiastic reception. The Institution has also given all possible assistance in the establishment of the proposed National Foundation on the Arts and the Humanities.

In science, which has always been the major preoccupation of the Smithsonian, nothing has more clearly demonstrated the consequences of neglecting areas of research than a recent development within the national oceanography program. A few years ago, the United States Government sought to expand the exploration of the oceans, for economic as well as scientific purposes. Under the Kennedy Administration, deep-sea research vessels were built and thousands of specimens were collected. But it was soon discovered that the results could not be properly interpreted because there were not enough trained biologists to identify the marine specimens. Because the Smithsonian had kept alive precisely the required field of biology, it was able to recruit and train specialists

in the work required. Today, oceanography is flourishing, and nowhere more intensively than at the Smithsonian itself, where nearly two score of scientists in such fields as zoology, botany, and paleontology contribute to the world-wide investigation.

Like marine biology, there are other scientific fields such as geophysics, anthropology, and descriptive biology which are too important to let languish until some chance stimulation comes along. Without new blood in the form of young men willing to enter these fields, they would, according to Secretary Ripley, grow extinct, "like a monastic order excommunicated by the Pope." In many such fields, the Smithsonian has long been a major source of support. Today, the Institution is reviving a precedent established in the days when young explorers learned the principles of field biology at the elbow of Spencer Baird. In its newly established Division of Education and Training, the Smithsonian is opening its doors to young scholars and becoming once more a university without classrooms. By a system of fellowship grants, it is drawing into its various scientific departments young university students—graduates and undergraduates—to work and study alongside the Institution's own three hundred professional scientists and scholars. It is hoped

that this will bring new life to fields of science that have not yet had their day in the sun. To the question of what is the use of more ichthyologists or ornithologists, the Smithsonian's answer is that science itself needs them. If these fields grew extinct, they would one day have to be re-created, and at incalculable cost.

In the field of descriptive biology, there is an ever more pressing urgency, for if it languishes, it may never be restored. Descriptive biology, the broad study of living things in their natural habitats (as distinguished from experimental laboratory research), faces the alarming prospect that the natural environment is disappearing from the face of the earth. A day may come when no portion of the globe will provide an example of nature unchanged by man. Smithsonian biologists predict that within thirty years many of the large animals will have disappeared even from the depths of the Amazon Basin jungles. To science, this means that the knowledge of the nature and evolution of animal species—and thus of human biological development—will be foreclosed forever. As a result, the Smithsonian is trying not only to encourage descriptive biology but also to preserve its very subject matter. An estate on Chesapeake Bay recently willed to the Smithsonian has been set aside as a special center for field

biology to be used for research and graduate education in conjunction with universities in the Washington area. The Institution hopes to set up or join in setting up biological preserves in such distant places as Honduras, Angola, and Panama (where the Canal Zone Biological Area already exists). Today, on the island of Dominica in the Caribbean, teams of Smithsonian biologists are engaged in investigations against the day when this relatively pristine island may succumb to irreversible transformation at the hands of man.

Because the Institution cannot singlehandedly preserve large patches of the earth's natural environment, it intends to enlist wherever possible the co-operation of foreign governments. In this sphere, the Smithsonian has the advantage of a long-standing international reputation for integrity and detachment. Since the days when the Smithsonian—with its expeditions and its generous exchange of publications—was the sole representative of official science in America, it has always been held in high esteem abroad. Quite recently, for example, the Organization of American States has co-operated with the Institution in bringing Latin American students to study at the Canal Zone Biological Area, thereby increasing the small number of trained Latin American field biologists

The Smithsonian's first Secretary, Joseph Henry, at center in the photograph at left, presides over a meeting of the National Academy of Sciences in a room of the old Smithsonian Building in the 1870's. In 1965, in an office that was once part of Henry's apartment in the Smithsonian Building, the eighth Secretary, S. Dillon Ripley, stands behind his desk (right) with bird specimens from his study collection in the foreground. The new direction set by Ripley for the Institution—that it be a "university that awards no degrees"—recalls the days of Henry when the Smithsonian was a focal point for American science. The renewed emphasis on research does not overshadow the "diffusion" of knowledge, however. Above, in the 1880's, books are loaded from the Smithsonian onto a cart. Today, over 650,000 copies of publications are being distributed each year.

PHOTOGRAPH BY ARNOLD NEWMAN

capable of studying the rapidly changing tropics. The Smithsonian also hopes to help Peru set up a field biology station in the untracked forest area east of the Andes which has already been set aside as a national preserve. As it explores the possibilities of international scientific co-operation, the Institution, to a greater extent than ever before, is fulfilling its international, as well as its national, responsibilities for the "increase and diffusion of knowledge among men." In the fields of its competence, it is helping to advise both foreign governments and American administrators of international co-operative programs on the over-all needs of science and how best they might be served. In the same spirit, the Smithsonian has recently taken over from the State Department the administration of foreign grants for archaeology and related disciplines.

This vigorous pursuit of excellence in so many fields of endeavor must find its justification in truly significant additions to knowledge. No organization of such size is immune from the risks of specialization. As each field has grown more complex and technical, it has tended to become a world of its own, out of contact with related disciplines. Though this may have certain advantages and short-term economies, such specialization is obviously unable to cope

with advanced problems that simultaneously touch upon many different disciplines. Increasingly, students of evolution, for example, must call on biochemists, astronomers, or other specialists to help them study the ancient environments from which present animal species evolved; modern oceanography draws on the skills of a half dozen different fields. The Institution is planning to inaugurate a center for advanced study in the old Smithsonian Building. The west wing will provide offices for visiting scholars, and a refectory and common room for these and other fellows and associates from Smithsonian bureaus and from nearby universities and Government research facilities. The scholars in residence will be chosen for their concern with subjects that draw naturally upon a wide range of fields, as, for instance, theoretical geophysics, art history and aesthetics, or the analysis of science as a social force. The intent today at the Smithsonian is to stimulate crosscurrents and interchange by reviving the concept of "the society of scholars" that had existed within its walls in the simpler days of Henry and Baird. For the Smithsonian, a community of scholars is the keystone in the Institution's role as a gathering place of the intellectually daring in all fields of knowledge.

INDEX

Italic page numbers indicate illustrations

ABBOT, CHARLES G., 65, 66, 67, 70, *70*
ADAMS, HENRY, 16, 31
ADAMS, JOHN QUINCY, 13, 15, 16, *17*, 62
AERODROME A, 60, *60*
AERODROME FIVE, *58*, 59
AERODROME SIX, *54-55*, 55
AGASSIZ, LOUIS, 23, 57, *57*
ALBERTI, 100, *100*
ALLEGHENY OBSERVATORY, 58
ALLEN, WILLIAM, 14
ANDREW MELLON COLLECTION, 95, 98, 104
ANTARCTICA, 31, 52
ANTHROPOLOGY, 38, 40, 44, 103, 123
ARAGO, FRANÇOIS, 24
ARCHAEOLOGY, 44, 45, 125
ARCTIC, 35, 37, 38
ARIZONA, 31, 34
ART: American, *10-11*, *22-23*, 24, *57*, 96-99, 103, *108*, 109, *109*, *110*, 111, *111*, 113, *113*; European, *94-95*, 95, 98 -100, *100*, 101, *101*, 103, 104, 106, 107, 110, 111, *112*; Impressionist, 100, *102*, 103, *103*, 111; Indian, 38, *38*, 39, *39*; Oriental, 99, 101, 106, *106*, *107*, 114, 116, *116*, 117, *117*; Postimpressionist, 103, 111; Western, *34*, 39, 97, 98. *See also* Painting, Sculpture
ARTS AND INDUSTRIES BUILDING, 37, *54*, 55, 77-79, 96, *96*, 103, 121
ASTROLABE, *74-75*, 75
ASTRONOMY, 16, 62, 67, 68, 125
ASTROPHYSICAL OBSERVATORY, 8, 16, 49, 56, 59, 62, 65, 67-69, 120, 122, *122*
ASTROPHYSICS, 58, 59, 61, 62
AUTOMOBILES, 87, 92, *92*

BACHE, ALEXANDER DALLAS, 57, *57*
BACON, FRANCIS, 9, *9*
BAIRD, SPENCER FULLERTON, 32, 33, 37, *37*, 43, 56, 59, 62, 76, 80, 123, 135
BALLOONS, 56, *56*, 57, 58, 68
BALTIMORE CLIPPER, *74-75*, 75
BANNISTER, HENRY, 35, 37
BARLOW, JOEL, 11, 12
BARRO COLORADO ISLAND, 44
BELL, ALEXANDER GRAHAM, 15, 59, 60, 61, *61*, 77
BELTER, J. H., 83, 90
BERENSON, BERNARD, 104
BIGELOW, ERASTUS BRIGHAM, 22, *22-23*
BIOLOGY: Descriptive, 123, 124; Marine, 44, 45, 48, 73, 84, 85, 122, 123
BLACKBURN, WILLIAM H., 50

BLANCHARD, THOMAS, 22, *22-23*
BLISS, BETTY TAYLOR, *82*, 83
BODHISATTVA, 114, 116, *116*, 117
BOGARDUS, JAMES, 22, *22-23*
BOTANY, 44, 47, 123
BRAUN, WERNHER VON, 67
BUCHANAN, JAMES, 83, 99
BUNSEN, 62
BURDEN, HENRY, 22, *22-23*
BUREAU OF AMERICAN ETHNOLOGY, 39, 40
BYRD, ADMIRAL RICHARD E., 52, 88

CANAL ZONE BIOLOGICAL AREA, 8, 44, *44*, 45, 124
CARBON-14, 73, *73*
CARIBBEAN SEA, 85, 124
CARMICHAEL, LEONARD, 79, 80, 88, *88*
CARNEGIE, ANDREW, 104
CATLIN, GEORGE, 39, 96, 97, *97*, 98, 113
CENTRAL AMERICA, 31, 45
CENTRAL PACIFIC, 47, 48
CHESTER DALE COLLECTION, 95, 103, 110
CHINA, 100, 106, 114, 116, 117
CHINOISERIE, 114
CHOATE, RUFUS, 14, 19, *19*, 23
CHOU DYNASTY, 114, 117
CHRYSLER, WALTER P., 52
COLORADO RIVER, 34, 39
COLT, SAMUEL, 22, *22-23*, 75
COMETS, 68, 69
COMMISSION OF FINE ARTS, 111
COOPER, PETER, 22, *22-23*
COPELAND, LUCIUS, 77, *77*
CORCORAN GALLERY OF ART, 99
CORLISS STEAM ENGINE, 77, *77*
COWAN, RICHARD S., 47, *47*
CURTISS, GLENN, 65

DALE, CHESTER, 110, 111. *See also* Chester Dale Collection
DARWIN, CHARLES, 38, 47, 78
DAVIS, ADMIRAL CHARLES, 57, *57*
DAVIS, STUART, 111, 113
DECATUR, STEPHEN, 108, *108*
DOMINICA ISLAND, 124
DOUGLAS, STEPHEN A., 19, 22
DUVEEN, LORD JOSEPH, 104, 107, 108

ECOLOGY, Marine, 122
EDISON, THOMAS, 14, *14*, 22, 76, 78
ELECTRICITY, 10, 21, 24, 26, 57, 89
ELECTROMAGNETISM, *15*, 21, 22, 24, 26, *26*, *27*, *27*, 93
ENTOMOLOGY, 47
ERICSSON, JOHN, 22, *22-23*
ETHNOLOGY, 32, 38-40, 43, 44, 122
EXOBIOLOGY, 69

FARADAY, MICHAEL, 21, 26
FIELD, CYRUS, 35
FILLMORE, ABIGAIL, *82*, 83
FINLEY, DAVID, 109, 110
FIRST LADIES, 79, 83, 99; Gowns of, *82*, 83, 87, 89
FLIGHT, 52, 55-61, 64, 65, 66, 67, 69, 121
FOSSILS, 10, 30, 38, 44, 47
FOUNDING FATHERS, 13, 90
FRANKLIN, BENJAMIN, 10, *10*, 22, 24
FREER, CHARLES LANG, 99-101, 106, *106*, 111, 114

FREER GALLERY OF ART, 100-101, 103, 114, 116
FREMONT, JOHN C., 31
FRICK, HENRY CLAY, 104, 106
FRICK COLLECTION, 106

GAINSBOROUGH, THOMAS, 99
GATLING GUN, 77, 84, *84*
GELLATLY, JOHN, 103, 106
GEOLOGY, 31, 32, 34, 38, 39, 45
GETTENS, RUTHERFORD J., 117
GODDARD, ROBERT H., 55, 64, *64*, 65, *65*, 66, 67, 69
GOODE, GEORGE BROWN, 76, 77-78, 79, 80, *81*, 85, 87, 89
GOODYEAR, CHARLES, 22, *22-23*
GOULD, BENJAMIN APTHORP, 57, *57*
GRAND CANYON OF THE COLORADO, 34, 35, 39

HARRISON, JOSEPH, 97, 98
HAYDEN, FERDINAND V., 32
HENRY, JOSEPH, 15, 19, 20, 21, *21*, 22, *22-23*, 24-27, 30-32, 35, 38, 43, 56, 57, *57*, 58, 62, 68, 69, 90, 92, 93, 120, 122, *124-125*, 125
HOE, RICHARD, 22, *22-23*
HOWE, ELIAS, 15, 22, *22-23*

INDIAN LANGUAGES, 39
INDIANS: Apache, 40; Blackfoot, 97, *97*; Calusa, 39; Hopi, 35; Mandan, 38, 96, *96*; Maya, 31; Paiute, 40, *40*; Shivwit, 40; Shoshoni, 39; Sioux, 31; Sitka, 38; Ute, 39; Winnebago, 40
IVES, LIEUTENANT JOSEPH, 34

JACKSON, ANDREW, 8, 113, *113*
JACKSON, WILLIAM HENRY, 31, *31*
JAPAN, 45, 100, 101, 106, 114, 116
JEFFERSON, THOMAS, 10, 12, 78
JOHNSON, ANDREW, 19
JOHNSTON, HARRIET LANE, 99, 109

KAIETEUR FALLS, *46*, 47
KENNEDY, JOHN F.: 121, 123; Center for the Performing Arts, 120
KENNICOTT, ROBERT, 35, *35*, 37, 56
KEY, FRANCIS SCOTT, 78, 79
KITTY HAWK, 60, 61, 67
KLEIN, WILLIAM, 73, *73*
KRESS, SAMUEL H., 95, 110. *See also* Samuel H. Kress Collection

LANGLEY, SAMUEL PIERPONT, 42, *42*, 50, 52, 55, 58, 59-62, *63*, 65, 69, 70, 76, 89
LEECH, DANIEL, 37, *37*
LESLIE'S ILLUSTRATED, 77, *77*
LEWIS AND CLARK, 75, 87
LIGHT, research on, 62, 70, 72, 73
LINCOLN, ABRAHAM, 57, *57*, 58, 90
LINCOLN, MARY TODD, *82*, 83
LINDBERGH, COLONEL CHARLES, 61, *61*
LOCOMOTIVES, *74-75*, 75, 77, 78, 89, 93
LOWE, THADDEUS S. C., 56, *56*, 57, 58

McCORMICK, CYRUS, 22, *22-23*
MACIE, ELIZABETH HUNGERFORD KEATE, 9
MAÑACH, PEDRO, *102*, 103
MANN, W. M., 52
MARSH, G. P., 15, 19
MEDICI, LORENZO DE', *94-95*, 95, 107

MEDICIS, MARIE DE, 100, *100*
MEIGS, GENERAL M. C., 37, *37*
MELLON, ANDREW W., 104, *105,* 106–110, 111, 113. *See also* Andrew Mellon Collection
METEORITES, 48, 49, *49,* 67, *67,* 68, 69, 121
METEOROLOGY, 48, 49, *49,* 57, 67, 119
METEORS, 68, 69
MICHELANGELO, 98
MICROPROBE, 49, *49, 118–119,* 119
MINERALOGY, 9, 10, 44, 77, 119
MINERVA, OWL OF, 2, *2*
MONITOR, 22
MOONWATCH, 68, 69, *69*
MORGAN, J. P., 98, 99, 104
MORSE, SAMUEL F. B., 22, *22–23,* 26, 76, 84. *See also* Telegraph
MORTON, WILLIAM, 22, *22–23*
MOTT, JORDAN, 22, *22–23*
MUSEUM OF HISTORY AND TECHNOLOGY: 76, 78–80, 82, 87–89, *89,* 90, 120; Dept. of Arts and Industries, 89; Dept. of Arts and Manufactures, 88; Dept. of Civil History, 88; Dept. of Cultural History, 82; Section of Musical Instruments, 87, *87,* 88; Dept. of Science and Technology, 88
MUSEUM OF NATURAL HISTORY: 42, *42, 43,* 44, 48, 84, 103, 119, 120, *120;* Office of Anthropology, 43, 44, 78; Div. of Birds, 44; Dept. of Botany, 44; Div. of Insects, 44, 45; Div. of Mammals, 44; Dept. of Mineral Sciences, 44; National Herbarium, 44; Dept. of Paleobiology, 44; Hall of the Sea, 120; Dept. of Zoology, 44

NAST, THOMAS, 111
NATIONAL ACADEMY OF SCIENCES, 57, *124–125,* 125
NATIONAL AIR AND SPACE MUSEUM, 120, *120–121,* 121
NATIONAL ARMED FORCES MUSEUM, 121
NATIONAL COLLECTION OF FINE ARTS, 87, *94–95,* 96, 97, 99, 108, 109, 111, *111,* 113, 120
NATIONAL GALLERY OF ART, *94–95,* 95, *98–99,* 99, 103, 104, 108–111
NATIONAL INSTITUTE, 14, 96
NATIONAL MUSEUM, 36, 37, *37,* 38, 43, 50, 77, 78, 80, 90
NATIONAL PORTRAIT GALLERY, 111, 113, 120
NATIONAL ZOOLOGICAL PARK, 50, *51,* 52, 120
NATURAL HISTORY, 10, 14, 15, 24, *28–29, 29–33, 35, 36,* 37–40, 42–45, 47–50, 52, 78
NEWTON, SIR ISAAC, 62
NORTHUMBERLAND (family), 9, 10
NOTT, ELIPHALET, 22, *22–23*

OCEANOGRAPHIC SORTING CENTER, 120, 122, *122*
OCEANOGRAPHY, 47, 48, 120, 122, *122,* 123, 125
ORNITHOLOGY, 47, 48, 88, 124
OWEN, ROBERT DALE, 14–15, 16, 19, *19*

PAINTING: (Angelico, Fra, and Filippo Lippi, Fra) "Adoration of the Magi," 110; (Bellini) "Portrait of a Condottiere," 110; (Birley) of Andrew Mellon, 104, *105;* (Bosch) "Death and the Miser," 100, *101;* (Botticelli) "Adoration of the Magi," 107; (Cézanne) "Still Life,"

94–95, 95; (Clouet) of Diane de Poitiers, 101, *101;* (Constable) "Wivenhoe Park, Essex," *94–95,* 95; (Copley) of Henry Laurens, 113, *113;* (Courbet) of the beach at Etretat, 103, *103;* (David) "Napoleon," *94–95,* 95; (Degas) of Mlle. Malo, 103, *103;* (Earl) of Andrew Jackson, 113, *113;* (Eyck, van) "Annunciation," 107; (Fisk) of George Catlin, 97, *97;* (Gauguin) "Fatata te Miti," 111; (Greco, El) "Laocoon," *94–95,* 95; (Grünewald) "The Small Crucifixion," *94–95,* 95; (Heem, de) "A Vase of Flowers," *94–95,* 95; (Herter) of Abraham Lincoln and founders of National Academy of Sciences, 57, *57;* (Homer) of bear hunters, *110,* 111; (Manet) "Old Musician," 111; (Moran) of Grand Canyon of the Yellowstone, 34, *34;* (Peale) of Benjamin Franklin, 10, *10;* (Picasso) of Pedro Mañach, *102;* 103; (Raphael) "Alba Madonna," 98, *98,* 107, "St. George and the Dragon," *94–95,* 95, 107; (Rembrandt) "The Mill," 98, *99,* 110, "Self-Portrait," *94–95,* 95, 107; (Renoir) "A Girl with a Watering Can," 111; (Ryder) "The Flying Dutchman," 109, *109;* (Schussele) "Men of Progress," 22, *22–23;* (Stuart) of Stephen Decatur, 108, *108,* of Mrs. Richard Yates, *94–95,* 95; (Thayer) of Mary Thayer, 109, *109;* (Titian) "Venus and Adonis," 110, "Venus with a Mirror," 104; (Vermeer) "A Woman Weighing Gold," 110, "Young Girl with a Flute," 110; (Walcutt) of Revolutionary patriots, 10, *10–11;* (Weyden, van der) "Portrait of a Lady," *94–95,* 95; (Whistler) "Venice, Second Series," 101
PALEONTOLOGY, 47, 48, 123
PARKER, PETER, 37, *37*
PATENT MODELS, 76, 82, 84, 90, *90,* 91, 92, *92, 93. See also* United States Patent Office
PEALE, CHARLES WILLSON, 10, 30, 113
PEALE, REMBRANDT, 30
PEARY, ADMIRAL, 88
PEIRCE, BENJAMIN, 57, *57*
PERCY (family), 8, 10
PHILADELPHIA CENTENNIAL EXPOSITION, 15, 76, *76,* 77, 80
PHOTOSYNTHESIS, 70, 73
PHOTOTROPISM, 70
PIERCE, JANE APPLETON, *82,* 83
POINSETT, JOEL, 14, 96
POLK, SARAH, *82,* 83
POLO, MARCO, 114, 116
POPE, JOHN A., 116, 117
POWELL, JOHN WESLEY, 39, 40, *41,* 56
PRIESTLEY, JOSEPH, 10, 12
PRINCETON UNIVERSITY, 19, 21, 24, 26
PROJECT CELESCOPE, 69
PUBLICATIONS (Smithsonian): 4, *4,* 20, 21, 23, 37, 38, 80, 87, 103, 123–125; *Contributions from the Museum of History and Technology,* 123; *Smithsonian Contributions to Knowledge,* 20, 21

REGENTS, BOARD OF, 15, 19, 20, 23, 37, 57, 79, 99, 100
RENWICK, JAMES, JR., 15, 19, 21
REYNOLDS, SIR JOSHUA, 99
RIPLEY, S. DILLON, 122, 123, 125, *125*
RIVER BASIN SURVEYS, 8, 43, *44–45,* 45
ROCKETS, 32, *54,* 55, 64, *64,* 65–67, 122
ROOSEVELT, THEODORE, 43, *43,* 44, 52, 60, 100, 108
ROSENWALD, LESSING J., 110. *See also* Rosenwald Collection

ROSENWALD COLLECTION, 110
ROYAL SOCIETY OF LONDON, 9, 10, 23
RUBENS, PETER PAUL, 108

SAMUEL H. KRESS COLLECTION, 100, 101
SATELLITES, 67–69, 122
SCIENCE, 8–11, 13, 22, 24, 90, 113, 120, 122, 123; research in, 13, 14, 16, 20, 22–24, 32, 33, 38, 48, 59, 66–70, 77, 87, 89
SCULPTURE: (Chinese) Bodhisattva, 114, *114;* (Houdon) "Diana," *94–95,* 95; (Japanese) Bodhisattva, 116, *116;* (Powers) "Greek Slave," 108, *108;* (Sant' Agata) "Hercules and Antaeus," 99, *99;* (da Settignano) bust of a little boy *94–95,* 95; (Verrochio) bust of Lorenzo de' Medici, *94–95,* 95
SHEPARD, ALAN, 55
SHIPS, MODELS OF, *74–75,* 75, 88
SMITHSON, JAMES, *6,* 7, 8, 9, *9,* 10–12, *12,* 14, 16, 19, 23, 24, 30, 77, 120
SMITHSONITE, 7
SOLAR RADIATION, 59, 65, 67, 70, 121, 122
SPACE CAPSULE, *54,* 55
SPACE RESEARCH, 48, 49, 56, 58, 59, 62, 64–69
SPIRIT OF ST. LOUIS, 61, *61*
SPUTNIK I, 68
SPUTNIK IV, 67, *67*
STAR-SPANGLED BANNER, 78, *78–79,* 79
STONE, EDWARD DURRELL, 120

TAFT, MRS. WILLIAM HOWARD, 79
TAXIDERMY, 21, *21*
TECHNOLOGY, 76–78, 83, 88, 89, 121
TELEGRAPH, 21, 22, *22–23,* 26, 35, 57, 76, 84
TRACKING STATIONS. *See* Moonwatch

UNION, THE, 14, 30, 31, 58
UNITED STATES CONGRESS, 8, 9, 12–16, 19, 23, 31, 37, 39, 43, 57, 77, 79, 89; 90, 92, 96, 97, 109, 111, 113, 121
UNITED STATES PATENT OFFICE, 14, 23, 30, 37, 67, 82, 90, 92, 111, 113, 120
UNITED STATES WEATHER BUREAU, 20, 57

WAGNER, 109
WALCOTT, CHARLES D., *60,* 61
WASHBURN, WILCOMB, 79, *79*
WASHINGTON, GEORGE, 10, 75, 78
WASHINGTON MUSEUM, 96
WEATHER FORECASTING, 20, 56–59, 62, 65, 68, *68,* 69
WETMORE, ALEXANDER, 88, *88*
WHIPPLE, FRED L., 49, 67–69
WIDENER, JOSEPH, 107, 110. *See also* Widener Collection
WIDENER, PETER A. B., 110
WIDENER COLLECTION, 95, 98, 99
WILKES, LIEUTENANT CHARLES, 14, 31
WILSON, HENRY, 57, *57*
WISE, JOHN, 56, 57
WORLD WAR I, 85, 121
WORLD WAR II, 45, 67
WRIGHT, JOSEPH, 9. *See also* Painting
WRIGHT, ORVILLE, 59, 60, *60–61,* 61, 65
WRIGHT, WILBUR, 59, 60, *60–61,* 61, 65
WRIGHT FLYER, 60, 65

ZOO. *See* National Zoological Park
ZOOLOGY, 44, 123

A NOTE ON THIS BOOK

This book was published by the Smithsonian Institution in association with the Editors of American Heritage Magazine, under the following editorial direction: for the Smithsonian Institution, Paul H. Oehser, Chief, Editorial and Publications Division; for American Heritage, Joseph J. Thorndike, Jr., Editor-in-Chief, and Richard M. Ketchum, Editorial Director of the Book Division.

The staff for this book was as follows: Editor, Charles L. Mee, Jr.; Art Director, Jack Newman; Copy Editor, Brenda S. Bennerup; Assistant Editor, Stephen W. Botein; Picture Editor, Douglas Tunstell; Editorial Assistants, Deborah Selkowitz and Sheila Scott.

All pictures, except as otherwise credited, come from the files of the Smithsonian Institution. Special photographs, as credited, were taken for this book by Arnold Newman with the assistance of Meredith Johnson of the Smithsonian Museum Service. The color plates on pages 38, 64, 85, and 98 are copyright © 1964, 1965, 1964, and 1964 by American Heritage Publishing Co., Inc.

Front Cover: The towers of the old Smithsonian Building, as seen from the southeast, were photographed from the top of the Arts and Industries Building by Arnold Newman.

Back Cover: The new flag of the Smithsonian bears the red demi-lion, in the upper left corner, from the coat of arms of Sir Hugh Smithson, James Smithson's father. The flag's wavy yellow border symbolizes the fact that Smithson, by reason of primogeniture, was not qualified to inherit his father's title. Centered in the blue field is a globe surrounded by the flames of the sun, representing the Institution's world-wide outposts and interests.